A JUST WAR NO LONGER EXISTS

A Just War No Longer Exists

The Teaching and Trial of Don Lorenzo Milani

Edited, Translated, and Annotated by

James Tunstead Burtchaell, C.S.C.

University of Notre Dame Press
Notre Dame, Indiana

Library of Congress Cataloging-in-Publication Data

Milani, Lorenzo.
    A just war no longer exists.

    Bibliography: p.
    1. Milani, Lorenzo — Trials, litigation, etc.
2. Trials (Political crimes and offenses) — Italy — Rome.
3. Conscientious objectors — Legal status, laws, etc. —
Italy.   I. Burtchaell, James Tunstead.   II. Title.
KKH41.M55J87   1988   343.45'0126   87-40347
ISBN 0-268-01191-5   344.503126

FOR
STANLEY HAUERWAS
WHO BELIEVES IN THESE THINGS

AND
STEPHEN MORIARTY
WHO HAS STOOD BY THESE THINGS

"On the subject of conscientious objection, I
would like to say that I think it is a sign of
maturity when people manage to accept another form of public service that is not military
service."

John Paul II

Contents

Introduction

Lorenzo Milani was born in Florence on 27 May 1923. His father, Albano Milani, was a rural landlord who died in March 1947, little more than a month before his son was to be ordained a priest. His mother, Alice Weiss, outlived her son and throughout his life remained a steadfast and constant influence upon him. Lorenzo had an older brother, Adriano, a physician, and a younger sister, Elena.

Fascist Italy was the scene of his childhood. The war was coming home to Italy in 1942 when Lorenzo completed his classical studies at secondary school. Instead of going to the university or to the military, he spent a year in art school. An intense interest in religious art, and then in liturgy, was a prelude to a religious conversion of sorts, which led him to the seminary in 1943. Whether because of the difficulties of the times, or his personal brilliance, he was obliged to study only four years before being ordained.

Calenzano is a run-down, urban neighborhood in an industrial zone that extends from Sesto Fiorentino to the rather ugly city of Prato, at a not-very-decent distance to the west of Tuscany's jewel, the city of Florence. Young Don Lorenzo's first assignment was to the parish of San Donato in Calenzano. His career was to be much influenced and protected by several older priests, wise in the ways of curias, and the pastor whom he served there as curate was one of them. Daniele Pugi was seventy-three years old when he had the livewire young cleric assigned to him (the assignment itself was the result of lobbying by another older patron, Don Raffaele Bensi, an influential parish priest and Lorenzo's mentor). Lorenzo's unconventional manner of thinking and his abrupt and impatient ways of expressing himself were not always to Don Raffaele's taste, but he tended to listen to the young man and give him a long leash. He protected him from the other clergy — not a few — who came to be unsettled by Lorenzo's unorthodox ways.

The new priest caught on immediately with the younger element in the parish. One of his first assignments was to teach the catechism classes that were obligatory in the local state school. This eventually led him to offer classes for young people who had already left school in their mid-teens to work in the factories. For them he eventually put together an after-hours institute that kept an already exhausted clientele up until near midnight. The instruction was not primarily religious. Milani met the needs and the interests of these people who were almost surprised themselves that their appetite for learning, far from being stifled by their blue-collar labor, was just now coming of age. They studied languages and politics and history, music and philosophy. He took to inviting professors and labor organizers, artists and politicians to come and give guest lectures.

Not all the parishioners warmed to Don Lorenzo's message. He himself admitted that the congregation at the more staid High Mass tended not to listen to anything he had to say from the pulpit. But the younger people, and those inclined toward liberal views on politics and economics, lionized him. At least some envy must have motivated the other clergy who resented his style, and word was regularly borne back to the archdiocesan curia about his deviant ministry.

Don Pugi was not long in his grave before a new assignment was found for his assistant. After seven years' pastoral experience Lorenzo was sent to a church of his own. It was, however, a church without a real parish, a church whose worshippers had already been told not to expect another incumbent. North of Florence, running along the ridge of the Apennines that thrust up from the Po valley beyond, the river Sieve has worn a gentle valley, the Mugello. On the north bank of that valley, by Monte Giovi, stands the modest town of Vicchio, about a dozen miles north of Florence as the bird flies. But Lorenzo was not assigned to Vicchio. He was assigned to Barbiana, a church in the woods on a hillside above the Mugello: a church too small to be a proper parish or, really, to have a proper pastor. Its incumbent went by the title of prior.

Scattered through the nearby woods were a few families who were just then in the process of giving up on their remote land and moving to the city for better work. Milani counted 230 persons in the settlement when he first came there. Before a decade was out he could count only eleven households, with thirty-nine members. When he arrived the area had no water, no postal service, no road, no electricity. It required no profound power of perception for him to realize that he had been put out to pasture. The archdiocese of Florence had in its gift no assignment more remote or less auspicious than the church of Barbiana. Yet it was here that Lorenzo Milani was to become one of the most celebrated and influential priests in all of Italy. He said nothing at all of his humiliating treatment — at the time — but later he liked to reminisce about what Simone Weil had said when she was unfairly discharged from her post as a teacher: "I have always expected that being dismissed would mark the high point of my academic career."

On his arrival he found his house full of the local children (for whom a change of priests must have been the most interesting news item in many a month). It was the children he took as his clientele. Their weary parents had little time to spare from scratching their living out of the hostile terrain. Another school was opened: partly with the help of the carloads of young people who came across from San Donato to visit their beloved Don Lorenzo on most weekends.

On days when the weather and her health permitted, a woman commuted up the mountain to teach the children in a one-room schoolhouse. After the elementary grades there was nothing available, and for years the youngsters had simply been disappearing into the factories. Lorenzo opened this school in his own house; during the warm months they sat outside in a nearby glade. Sometimes there were six students; sometimes there were fourteen or eighteen or more. Parents in other hamlets began to send their children to the School of Barbiana. Sometimes the parents were unwilling and had to be cajoled. Sometimes it was the pupils who were reluctant, and they came under threat. Very young boys and the occasional girl sometimes walked miles along through the woods to and from Barbiana each day. When the settlement was down to only thirty-nine inhabitants, the school counted twenty-nine pupils. The families that remained, and that had taken in outsiders to board, had stayed only so that the children could study. Some of those parents had to walk nearly five miles down the mountain to catch a train for an hour-and-a-half journey in to their jobs in Florence, and then turn around and make the return journey late into the evening.

Meanwhile, back on Mount Giovi, Lorenzo and his scholars were reading Plato, Shakespeare, Manzoni, and the Gospels. They were studying French, Spanish, German, English and Arabic. Eventually Milani sent them off on annual excursions to perfect the languages they had been studying — when they were only fifteen or sixteen years old, and sometimes as young as thirteen. They were studying geometry and building themselves an astrolabe. They were following the score of a Mozart symphony and pounding out the beat of Beethoven. Don Lorenzo's friends began to trek up the hillside (his first year he had rallied all the youngsters to extend the road another kilometer or so up to the church) to teach whatever they knew: labor relations, statistics, pottery. Visitors began to come, to the point where it was not unusual for sixty-five to sit down to lunch at the school, and for several dozen extra overnight guests to have to be bedded down throughout the houses. Each year his scholars journeyed into the town for several days to take the national examinations, and years passed without a single pupil failing in a single subject.

Lorenzo Milani was never in robust health. Since seminary days he had been bothered by serious digestive problems. He seemed at one time to have a heart murmur. He survived pneumonia and tuberculosis. In 1960 he showed the first symptoms of a much more ominous disorder, lymphogranuloma. As this progressively worsened, he contracted leukemia. His last years were crippled by disease, to the point where it was common for him to teach and direct the school and receive visitors from either a couch or his bed.

While his body yielded gradually to weakness, his character took on a tougher tone. Lorenzo was a truculent man, and although until his last days he rarely stood up for his own good name or interests, he was roused to wrath on behalf of anyone he thought to be an underdog. A local resident who refused to let the inhabitants pipe water to their houses from an unused spring on his property; a group of city slickers who bilked most of the households in a scam to enlarge the photographs of their deceased relatives for exorbitant prices and with fine print in the contracts; a minor government official who doggedly refused to lend an educational vehicle to take Milani's pupils to France; a cement factory that would take no responsibility to help a homeless woman and children whose breadwinner had been killed on the job: these were typical targets of his wrath. And Don Lorenzo did not give up until his adversary was defeated. Once the Vicar General of the archdiocese sent a telegram advising him not to attend a civic gathering in another town. Milani went on a three-month preaching strike, which ended only when his superior came all the way out to the hamlet, tried to explain to the group of teenagers why he had sent the telegram, and left a contribution to the school. Another strike coerced a negligent landowner into fixing a backed-up sewer that was defiling the neighborhood. Milani was driven to teach the poor how to stand up to the people in power without being intimidated. And he gave them an intrepid example himself.

One criticism that irritated him more than most was that he fostered alienation between socio-economic classes. Lorenzo came from a comfortable family, and though he frequently confessed that he was out of cash, his family was able and willing to subsidize him from the ample income on their farm lands. He was himself a child of the bourgeoisie. As a young man he had just a touch of priggishness. But before many years had passed he was building chapels and roads with his own hands, and burning those hands with lime in the process. He refused to take contributions from the public for his prescribed priestly attentions, but with increasingly astute pragmatism he managed the parish's property assets to yield enough to help with the bills. When he was out of sorts he sometimes snubbed the affluent and the educated, and treated them to offhand insults that tried their devotion to him.

Yet it was not in him to treat the poor that roughly. With them he became antagonized only when they fawned or truckled. To some young people who were working their way up in the labor unions, he angrily insisted that they should never dress in suits and ties the way their management counterparts did, and that they should refuse to shake hands with executives, but greet only their chauffeurs and doormen. He was a classist in that his driving sense of justice always framed itself in terms of haves and have-nots, and he was far more prone to see the sins of the former. He was so piercing in his depiction of mistreatment by those in power that he gave new voice and clarity to the resentment of their victims, and made it the more difficult for the powerful to see themselves well enough to think better of what they were doing.

Milani was a complex man. Though he was im-
placably antagonized by authority figures, he was himself
rigorously authoritarian. He was very fond of citing the
First Article of the Italian Constitution: "Italy is a democratic Republic founded on labor. Sovereignty belongs
to the people who exercise it in the manner and within
the limits laid down by the Constitution." "Sovereignty"
was as good a word as any to describe the character trait
he wished most of all to engender in his boys and girls.
Yet at Barbiana he was clearly sovereign, running the
school and governing the consciences of his youngsters
with undisputed rule.

To his colleagues he had to be a religious mystery.
His mother, whom he held in immense respect, was a
Jewess. There had been little if any religious practice
in his immediate family. He dealt easily with Communist
party officials (most of whom had been excommunicated
by Vatican decree shortly after his ordination, and many
of whom were childhood acquaintances) and with partisans of the extreme right. The Christian Democrats he
had a hard time telling apart from the old Fascists. In
an Italy where the battle-lines were drawn, and where
the clergy and the majority party propped one another
up and saw adversaries on all sides, Lorenzo Milani
moved between the barricades with an almost serene
naïveté. Few would have been surprised by his (private)
remark that the right patron for his school was Socrates
rather than Jesus.

He had been at San Donato only a few years when
he began to work on the manuscript of a book that was
published eight years later: *Esperienze pastorali*. What he
intended was an enthusiastic and analytic account of
what he was learning as a priest. What most of his fellow

8

clerics read there was contempt for the only style of ministry with which they were comfortable. Milani saw Italy as spiritually withered for want of spiritual and attentive shepherding. The book was forced off the bookstore shelves by Vatican decree the Christmas after it was released.

It was with his fellow clergy that his most anguished conflicts always occurred. As a rookie he learned that disgruntled clergy were bad-mouthing him to his superiors. He reciprocated by not frequenting clerical gatherings, and by drifting away from many of the ordinary priests of the area. He served under two prelates: Elia Della Costa and Ermenegildo Florit. When either of them dealt with him in a way that he regarded as irresponsibly uninformed — either directly or through some functionary — Don Lorenzo would characteristically fire off a great salvo in the form of a lengthy, documented letter, excruciatingly logical and ending in only two alternatives. His superior could either admit that he had been a fool, or rage inwardly at this disgraced priest who gave him no way of saving face. The correspondence from his superiors suggests that this discredited, exiled priest was able to unnerve both of the Cardinal Archbishops of Florence.

Sometimes he would receive a word to the wise from an old friend like Don Bensi, to be less aggressive. Sometimes he would be sent an episcopal secretary or an auxiliary bishop to look to his wants and to show a supportive face. In Milani's last years the Cardinal several times sent what he thought to be a frank and extensive letter — in the Milani style — along with checks to cover mounting expenses, and Milani would take the letters as intensified insults. Somehow his exchanges with authorities always went bad.

The papacy itself may be an exception. The Vatican decree banning his first book was dated after the death of Pope Pius XII, but must have been prepared during his pontificate. John XXIII, who succeeded to the papacy in 1958, spoke warmly and agreeably of Milani, who was then becoming well known, but suggested to a mutual acquaintance that a little prudence might help. Milani noted the remark without rancor. Later he was puzzled by a courtesy letter from the Pope's secretary, probably a goodwill gesture that did not speak strongly enough to suit Lorenzo's strong craving for appreciation. By the time Paul VI came into office in 1963, deteriorating health and festering controversy rivaled one another to harry Lorenzo. When Paul sent word that he thought it indiscreet to have his letter of response to the military chaplains published in a Communist newspaper, Milani remarked tartly that it was only because all the Catholic press refused to carry it. But in the months of his worst sickness and of the criminal prosecution, the Pope was repeatedly sending him checks and moral support. It is tragic that these expressions of solidarity, which are hardly typical from a Pope to the most controversial priest in Italy, should have riled Lorenzo rather than assuaged him.

He was obsessed by the failure of his superiors to stand up for him, to praise his work that everyone else was admiring, to say out loud that he was a faithful and devoted servant. In his last days he was beside himself with anger at the hedged and, as he felt, half-hearted gestures from his ecclesiastical superiors.

This was the talented, proud, individualist, impatient, prophetic, touchy priest whose climactic adventure was to be a public debate — national at first, and since then international — over conscientious objection to the bearing of arms. At a time when that had been a topic of heated controversy in his country, where no such legal exemption from military service was legally recognized, Lorenzo Milani entered into the public quarrel and found himself the defendant in a criminal prosecution for having incited young Italians to defy the law. It would draw from his pen and from those of other parties to the controversy some statements which deserve to be remembered in the annals of the many eloquent men and women who spoke to that issue in those troubled years. The principal documentation from that debate, and of the criminal prosecution which pursued Milani even on his deathbed, is the substance of this book.

Every Italian young man expected to face conscription and to serve a term in the armed forces. This had to be a concern of the young boys schooled at Barbiana. On one of their group excursions to Florence Lorenzo was distressed to have a pupil arrested and held by the police for having given false information for his conscription files. At school one of his projects was to prepare his boys for careers as social activists, and to teach them techniques and tactics for standing up to those in a position to coerce them. Of this he wrote:

> Naturally we will not limit this to dealing with police, but also with so-called "military superiors." Today this must be at the price of conscientious objection: they have to speak out and to act in ways that would be approved by tomorrow's legislator, in the ways they deal with officers: not letting themselves be humiliated simply for the sake of discipline, not doing squat-walks or suffering physical abuse or taking

laxatives. I have heard instances of all four of these abuses from boys who did military training.

A policeman stopped me once when I needed to drive past a bicycle race. I stopped because I was afraid I might run over someone or be run over myself. But is it legal to barricade off a public road for hours to please some fanatics, and thereby to inconvenience some others who aren't fanatics? (That goes for processions too.) And if it isn't legal, how do you handle the authorities? In what terms does one refuse obedience, etc.?[1]

When the first of his boys was called up for military service he did not want to go, but Milani persuaded him to acquiesce. They agreed beforehand however that the boy should "conscientiously object" to any orders that he regarded as evil. The boy was in the barracks only a few days before being sent home as undesirable.

The truculent prior naturally saw military authorities as an archetype of the intimidating and awesome power he was giving his whole life to overthrow. He was particularly resentful of its ability to incapacitate the poor. His long acquaintance with the Gozzini family made him all the more attentive when young Giuseppe Gozzini refused to answer his conscription call and was sentenced to prison by a court martial. Milani's long-time friend, Father Ernesto Balducci, published a statement in support of the young man and was promptly convicted himself of incitement to crime. Italy then had no laws which would permit conscripts to plead conscientious objection to armed service. Milani put his fellow Tuscan priests on public notice that they had been poor in their support of their plucky and outspoken colleague.

Two years later the Prior of Barbiana was drawn into such a controversy himself. The documents presented here tell the story by themselves. In the fading days of his energy and of his life, when he was more estranged from those he resented, and more disabled by physical pain and weakness, than ever in his whole life, Lorenzo Milani and his ragtag troop of peasant teenagers swiftly set down in two breathless manifestos as eloquent a conviction about authentic patriotism and about repugnance to warfare as has been crafted in our time. It is beholden to Gandhi, and it is worthy of him. Typically and appropriately it pits Lorenzo Milani against fellow priests.

Haled into court by the complaints of indignant war veterans, Milani was made to stand trial for what he had published. He was acquitted by the court of first instance of the crimes of which he was accused: incitement to crime and advocacy of crime. Under Italian law that acquittal was subject to appeal, and eventually it went to court again, with a decision this time to the contrary. But Lorenzo Milani by then had passed to an even higher jurisdiction: he died four months before, on 27 June 1967. His publisher and codefendant was left to answer to the Italian judiciary. Knowing that he was dying, and that he had had his say, Don Lorenzo left the judiciary to ponder his case without much further attention. His last days — and the last days of his beloved youngsters with him — were devoted to the completion of a last book, this time on education. That is a book that continues to be read. Yet this present book, the documents from the Case of Don Lorenzo Milani, may in years to come remain as his most enduring valedictory.

Barbiana is deserted now, visited only by the occasional alumnus who climbs the hill to visit the grave of

the prior. His trenchant and unnerving thoughts, however, continue to remain in print. Books by him, and
published correspondence, include:

> *Esperienze pastorali* (Florence: Libreria Editrice Fioren-
> tina, 1958)
> *Lettera a una professoressa*, by the Scuola di Barbiana
> (Florence: Libreria Editrice Fiorentina, 1967)
> *Lettere di Don Lorenzo Milani*, ed. Michele Gesualdi
> (Milan: Mondadori, 1970)
> *Lorenzo Milani: lettere alla mamma, 1943–1967*, ed. Alice
> Milani Comparetti (Milan: Mondadori, 1973)

Don Lorenzo's youngsters are scattered. Many have
become teachers. Quite a few have become labor union
officers. They are the closest disciples who literally sat
at the feet of the teacher. Through this translation I have
endeavored to widen somewhat the circle of those who
could listen to the voice of the man whose body lies buried
in the woods on the slopes of Mount Giovi, but whose
spirit still has much to say to young people, and others
not so young.[2]

This book is substantially a translation of documents
that are now on the public record. Some of them were
printed, albeit with a number of errors, in *L'Obbedienza
non è più una virtù: documenti del processo di Don Milani*
(Florence: Libreria Editrice Fiorentina, [1969]). I am
responsible for having gathered, verified, translated, and
presented all the documents here, for having written the
introduction, and for having supplied all of the footnotes.

I am grateful to the following persons who were of help
in my preparation of this manuscript. Signor Luca Pavolini, of the central committee of the Italian Communist

Party, accorded me an informative interview. Francuccio Gesualdi, once one of Don Lorenzo's favorite pupils, has been generous in corresponding with me. Acknowledgment is due several research libraries for their resources: at Cambridge University, the University Library and the Squire Law Library; in London, the Institute for Advanced Legal Studies; in Rome, the Biblioteca Nazionale, the clerk's office of the Court of Appeal of Rome, and the archive of *L'Unita*, of the Italian Communist Party. A visiting fellowship from Saint Edmund's House in Cambridge Univeristy offered me gracious hospitality during the time I did the work. James Langford, director of the Notre Dame Press, has offered me encouragement along the way and has generously accepted this book for publication, my first with our own University publisher.

An Order-of-the-Day Issued by
Retired Military Chaplains in Tuscany

The entire controversy which embroiled the last months of Lorenzo Milani's life was initiated by a short news item that appeared in the local Florentine press one day in 1965. The subject of conscientious objection had been active in the previous year or so, and several Catholic clergy had become vocal supporters of Catholic young men who had chosen to accept prosecution and imprisonment rather than accept conscription and bear arms. This eventually led a group of ex-chaplains to express their indignation.

On the anniversary of the Reconciliation between the Church and the State of Italy, the retired military chaplains residing in Tuscany gathered yesterday, at the Institute of the Holy Family on Via Lorenzo il Magnifico.

At the conclusion of their business, on motion of Don Alberto Cambi, in the chair, the following order-of-the-day was agreed upon:

The retired military chaplains in Tuscany, in the spirit of the recent national convention of their association which took place in Naples, offer respectful and brotherly acknowledgment to all of Italy's Fallen. It is their hope that finally, in God's name, there be an

16

end to all differentiation between soldiers of any campaign or any military unit who laid down their lives in sacrifice for the sacred ideal of Fatherland.

As for what some call "conscientious objection," the chaplains consider it to be an insult to the Fatherland and to its Fallen, as something alien to the Christian commandment of love, and as an expression of cowardice.

The assembly concluded with a prayer on behalf of all the Fallen.[3]

—— II ——

Letter of Don Lorenzo Milani to the Military Chaplains of Tuscany Who Signed the Communiqué of 11 February 1965[4]

Within less than a month Milani and his pupils composed a reply to the chaplains' communiqué which Milani signed, had printed, and sent round to all the local clergy. He also sent it to a number of newspapers and magazines. It appeared in its entirety in La Rinascita, *a magazine published in Rome by the Communist Party of Italy.*

For some time now I have wanted to have one of you speak to my youngsters about your life. It is a life which the children and I do not understand.

Still, we would have wanted to make an effort to understand, and especially to ask you how you have coped with some of the practical problems of military life. But I did not act soon enough to organize this meeting between you and my school.

My preference would have been to talk of these things privately, but now that you have taken up the issue publicly, and in a newspaper, I have no choice but to address these questions to you publicly.

First: why have you insulted citizens whom we and

many other people admire? No one, as far as I am aware, had raised a voice against you. Possibly the simple consistency of their heroic Christian example aggravates some internal insecurity within yourselves.

Second: why have you used, in an offhand and undefined way, words that are oversized for you?

Before you reply, keep in mind that public opinion today is more mature than it used to be, and will not be satisfied either by silence on your part, or by a vague retort that ignores our specific questions. Sentimental slogans or vulgar insults directed at conscientious objectors or at me are not arguments. If you have arguments I will be happy to acknowledge them, and to correct myself if in the impulse of my writing I should have expressed myself unfairly.

I shall not discuss here the idea of Fatherland as such. It involves a distinction with which I do not agree. If you persist in claiming the right to divide the world into Italians and foreigners, then I must say to you that, in your view of things, I have no Fatherland. I would then want the right to divide the world into disinherited and oppressed on one side, and privileged and oppressors on the other. One group is my Fatherland; to me, the others are foreigners. And if, without being disciplined by the church, you have the right to teach that it can be a moral thing — even heroic — for Italians and foreigners to tear each other to pieces, I claim the right to say that then the poor can and should take up arms against the rich.

At least in the choice of weapons we enjoy the advantage. The arms which you condone are horrible devices of war to kill, to mutilate, to destroy, to make widows and orphans. The only weapons I condone are noble and bloodless: the strike and the ballot.

We have, then, very different ideas. I can respect yours if you manage to justify them in light of the Gospel or the Constitution. But you too must respect the ideas of others. Especially if they are people who pay for their ideas in person.

You will surely agree that the word "Fatherland" is often put to improper use. Frequently it serves simply as a pretext to dispense oneself from reflection, or from the study of history, or from making choices, on occasion, between the Fatherland and even nobler values.

In this letter I do not wish to appeal to the Gospel. It is all too easy to demonstrate that Jesus was opposed to violence and that he did not accept even legitimate self-defense, per se. I shall refer instead to the Constitution:

> Article 11: "Italy condemns war as an instrument of aggression against the liberties of other peoples. . ."[5]
> Article 52: "Defense of the Fatherland is a sacred duty of the citizen."

Let us use this standard to take the measure of the wars to which the Italian people have been summoned throughout the one century of our history.

If we should find that the history of our army is implicated in offenses against the Fatherlands of others, you then ought to clarify for us whether in those cases the soldiers should have obeyed, or should have raised the objections presented by their consciences. And then you ought to explain who *defended* the Fatherland and its honor more: those who objected or those who by their obedience made our Fatherland odious in the eyes of the entire civilized world? Spare us the high-flown or evasive speeches. Get down to the facts. Tell us just what you

20

have taught the soldiers. Obedience at all costs? What if the orders were for the bombardment of civilians, a reprisal mission against a defenseless village, the summary execution of partisans, the use of atomic or bacteriological or chemical weapons, torture, the execution of hostages, drum-head trial of mere suspects, decimation (selecting every tenth soldier of the Fatherland and then shooting him to strike fear into the other soldiers of the Fatherland), a war of obvious aggression, an order from an officer in revolt against the sovereign people, or the repression of public demonstrations?

These actions and many others of the sort are the daily bread of every war. When they took place in front of your eyes either you lied or you kept silent. Or do you wish us to believe that you have been insisting on the truth time after time, eye-to-eye with your "superiors," in defiance of prison or death? If you still have your lives and your promotions, it must be a sign that you have raised no objections at all. In any case you have demonstrated conclusively by your communiqué that you have not the slightest notion of the concept of conscientious objection.

You cannot avoid making a judgment on the events of yesteryear if you wish to be — as you should be — the moral mentors of our soldiers. To begin with, the Fatherland — we, that is — are paying you or have paid you for that very purpose. And if we maintain a very expensive army (one trillion lire a year), it is only so that it can defend both the Fatherland and the high values which that concept comprises: sovereignty of the people, freedom, justice. And that is all the more reason why, with history books in hand, you should have educated our soldiers for objection rather than for obedience.

Throughout these one hundred years of history they have known all too little objection. To their shame and that of the world, they have known all too much obedience.

Let us page through history together. In each instance you must tell us which side represented the Fatherland; which direction we should have fired in; when it was right to obey; and when, to object.

1860. An army of Neapolitans, consumed by their patriotic zeal, tried to drive into the sea a handful of brigands which was attacking their Fatherland. Among those brigands there were various Neapolitan officers who were deserters from their Fatherland. It was, to be precise, the brigands who won. Today every one of them has a statue in some Italian piazza commemorating him as a hero of the Fatherland.[6]

One hundred years later history repeats itself: Europe is at our gates. The Constitution hastens to greet her: "Italy agrees to the necessary limitations of sovereignty . . ."[7] Our children will laugh at your concept of Fatherland, just as we all now laugh at the Fatherland of the Bourbons. And our grandchildren will laugh at that of Europe. The uniforms of the soldiers and of the military chaplains will be on display only in museums.

The war following 1866 was another war of aggression. In fact, we made an alliance with the most truculent, war-mongering nation in the world to collaborate in a joint attack on Austria.[8]

The wars of 1867–1870 against the Romans were surely wars of aggression. The Romans were not very fond of their civil Fatherland, and they did little to defend it. But neither were they fond of their new Fatherland which was invading them, nor did they rise up to hasten its victory. As Gregorovius explained it in his diary: "The uprising scheduled for today has been cancelled due to rain."[9]

In 1898 the "Gallant" King bestowed the Grand Military Cross on General Bava-Beccaris for his services in a war it is good for us to remember. The enemy was a crowd of beggars who were waiting for some soup outside a convent in Milan. The General hit them with a bombardment of cannons and mortars simply because the rich (yesterday just like today) demanded the privilege of not paying taxes. They wanted to raise the tax on cornmeal, to shift more burden onto the poor, and off their own shoulders. They got what they wanted. There were eighty dead, and countless wounded. Among the soldiers there was not a single man wounded, nor a single man who objected. When their army service was over they went home to eat polenta. Not much of it, though, for it had become more expensive.[10]

Then their officers had them shouting for "Savoy!" when they sent them twice (1896 and 1935) to invade a distant and peaceful people who were in no way threatening the borders of our Fatherland. These were the only black people who had not previously been wasted by the plague of European colonialism.[11]

When whites and blacks are fighting, are you with the whites? Is it not enough to impose on us the Italian Fatherland? Do you also want to impose the White Race Fatherland? Are you the kind of priests who read *La Nazione*? Read it carefully, for it is a newspaper that considers the life of one white worth more than the lives of one hundred blacks. You have seen the coverage it gave to the killing of sixty whites in the Congo, but it forgot to describe the appalling slaughter

23

of blacks and to identify the whites who are directing it all from Europe.

The same for the war in Libya.[12]

Then we come to 1914. Italy attacks Austria of which, this time, it had been an ally.

Was Battisti a patriot or a deserter?[13] It is a minor detail, but one you should clear up if you want to talk about Fatherland. Did you tell our boys that that was a war we could have avoided? That Giolitti knew for certain that he could obtain gratis what he ended up obtaining with 600,000 deaths? That the overwhelming majority of the Chamber of Deputies was ready to support him (450 out of 508)?[14] Was it then the Fatherland that did the calling to arms? And if it did issue the call, was it not perhaps to a "useless carnage"? (The expression comes, not from a cowardly conscientious objector, but from a canonized Pope.)[15]

In 1922 the Fatherland needed to be defended against attack. But the army did not defend it. It stood in wait for the orders that never came.[16] If their priests had educated them to be guided by *conscience* instead of by "blind, swift, and absolute" *obedience*, how many sorrows might have been spared the Fatherland and the world (50,000,000 dead).[17] As it turned out, the Fatherland fell into the power of a handful of criminals who violated every law, human and divine, and, with their mouths full of the word "Fatherland," brought the country to catastrophe. In those tragic years, the priests who had nothing but the sacred word "Fatherland" in their minds and mouths, who never desired to deepen the sense and resonance of that expression, who spoke as you now speak — those priests did a pathetic injury to the Fatherland (and, be it said in passing, they also dishonored the church).

In 1936 fifty thousand Italian troops found themselves embarked on a new and infamous aggression. They had all filled out the statutory "volunteer's card" in order to join in an attack on the hapless Spanish people.[18]

They ran to the aid of a general who was a traitor to his Fatherland, a rebel against his lawful government and his sovereign people.[19] With the help of Italy, and at the cost of a million and a half lives, he succeeded in obtaining what the rich wanted: wage controls without price controls, abolition of strikes, of unions, of political parties, of every civil and religious liberty. Still today, in defiance of the rest of the world, that revolting general imprisons, tortures, kills (even garrots) whoever is guilty of having defended the Fatherland then or of trying to do so now. Without the obedience of the Italian "volunteers" this would never have happened.

If, in those sad times, there had not been Italians on the other side as well, none of us could look a Spaniard in the eye today.[20] Those Italians were, to be precise, rebels and exiles from their own Fatherland. They were people who had objected. Have you said to your soldiers where their duty would lie if they should have a general like Franco? Have you explained that officers who disobey their sovereign, the people, must not be obeyed?

Then, from 1939 onwards there was a landslide: the Italian soldiers attacked six other Fatherlands, one after the other, which had certainly not attacked their own: Albania, France, Greece, Egypt, Yugoslavia, Russia.[21] It was an Italian war that had two fronts: one against the democratic system; the other, against the socialist. They were and still are the two noblest political systems mankind has yet been given. One represents the highest attempt of humankind to give, already on this earth, liberty and human dignity to the poor. The other represents the highest attempt of humankind to give, already on this earth, justice and equality to the poor.

Don't go to the effort of answering by accusing these systems of their respective faults and mistakes. We know that these are human things. Tell us instead what we were offering in their place: without a doubt the worst political system that unscrupulous oppressors have ever been able to dream up. It was a rejection of every moral value, and every liberty except for the rich and for the perverse. A rejection of every justice and of all religion. Propaganda of hate and extermination of innocents. One result, among others, was the extermination of the Jews, the Fatherland of the Lord, dispersed and suffering across the world.

What befell the Fatherland through all that? And what could be the meaning of Fatherlands at war now, after that last war when it was really ideologies, and not Fatherlands, that stood in opposition?

At last, during this hundred years of Italian history there was also one "just" war . . . if such a thing exists. It was the only war in which other Fatherlands were the aggressors and ours was on the defensive: the war of resistance by the partisans. On one side were civilians; on the other, military. One one side they were soldiers who had obeyed; on the other, soldiers who had objected. Which of the two forces, in your judgment, were the rebels and which were the regulars? It is a notion that needs to be clear if you are going to talk about Fatherland. In the Congo, for instance, who are the rebels?

Eventually, thank God, our Fatherland lost the unjust war which it had unleashed. The Fatherlands attacked by our Fatherland succeeded in driving back our troops.

Certainly we owe those troops our respect. They were hapless farmers or workers who were turned into aggressors by military obedience. The same military obedience that you chaplains glorify without a single *distinguo* to relate it to St. Peter's question: "Is it God or men that we ought to obey?"[22] And yet you heap injury on a few courageous men who have ended up in prison for doing what St. Peter did.

In many civilized countries (more civilized, in this regard, than our own) the law respects them by allowing them to serve the Fatherland in another way. They are asking to make greater sacrifices for the Fatherland, not lesser ones. They are not to blame if in Italy similar men have no choice but to serve their Fatherland idly in prison.

There is, as a matter of fact, a law in Italy which does recognize conscientious objection. It is the very Concordat which you were intending to commemorate.[23] Its third article sanctions the outright conscientious objection of bishops and priests.

As for other objectors, the church has yet made no pronouncement either for them or against them. The human sentence imposed on them is simply that they have disobeyed the law of men, not that they are cowards. Who has authorized you to add insult to that injury? When you call them cowards, do you ever recall anyone saying that cowardice is the exception and heroism the rule?

Hold back your insults. Perhaps tomorrow you will find that these men are prophets. Admittedly, the place of prophets is in prison, but it is not very becoming to take sides with whoever put them there.

If you tell us that you have chosen the vocation of

chaplains in order to help the wounded and the dying, that is an idea we can respect. Gandhi as a young man did the same. When he was older he harshly disavowed that error of his youth. Have you read his life?

But if you tell us that the refusal to defend oneself and one's own according to the example and the commandment of our Lord is "alien to the Christian commandment of love," then you are not aware of what Spirit you belong to! What kind of language are you using? How can we listen to you if you use words without measuring their meaning? If you do not wish to honor the suffering of the objectors, have the goodness at least to be still!

Our hopes are the contrary of what you hope for. Our hope is that finally there be an end to all discrimination by the *Fatherland* toward soldiers of any campaign or any military unit who gave their lives in sacrifice for the sacred ideals of justice, freedom, and truth.

Let us respect suffering and death, but let us not dangerously confuse the young people who look to us, about good and evil, about truth and error, about the death of an aggressor and the death of his victim.

Let us say, if you will: we pray for those unfortunate people who have, through no fault of their own, been poisoned by a propaganda of hatred, and have sacrificed themselves for a misunderstood ideal of Fatherland, while unwittingly trampling underfoot every other noble human ideal.

Don Lorenzo Milani

"Conscientious Objection is not Cowardice"
A Letter from a Group of Priests
and Catholic Laymen

At the very same time a group of Catholic activists, led by Don Bruno Borghi, sent their reply to the chaplains as a letter to the editors of several journals. Their statement, unlike that of Milani, was carried in several journals. Rinascita *carried it in the same issue in which Milani's statement was printed.*

Dear Editor:

La Nazione has published, on 22 February 1965, an order-of-the-day adopted by the retired military chaplains resident in Tuscany. After paying tribute to all those who have fallen for Italy and calling for an end to discrimination and division with respect to the soldiers who have fallen "for the sacred ideal of Fatherland," the chaplains have informed us that "as for what some call 'conscientious objection,' " they "consider it to be an insult to the Fatherland and to its Fallen, as something alien to the Christian commandment of love, and as an expression of cowardice."

Declarations uttered from that kind of pulpit call to

29

mind several recent events. A position taken by a group of "authorized theologians" on the subject of conscientious objection, combined with the silence of those whose duty it is to assert the freedom of Catholics in this issue, could lead people to imagine that the controversy has been conclusively settled, and that whoever chooses to be an objector is now not only exposed to the criminal law as a threat to the state, but is also outside the church.

But this is certainly not the case, at least as regards the church. And we nourish the hope that the Italians, like other civilized nations, will see fit to provide themselves with a law that will authorize conscientious objection.

There is, however, more to be said. The chaplains' declarations, and the chaplains themselves, deserve a reply.

In matters this serious one has the right to know the theological and moral principles on which the chaplains are taking their stand. We do not see how it is an insult to our own Fatherland to love those who belong to another. Nor can we understand how conscientious objection can be alien to the Christian commandment of love, if we are ordered in the gospel to love even our enemies, which is precisely what the conscientious objectors are urging us to do. How can one claim that conscientious objection is an expression of cowardice, when the objector is ready to pay in person for loyalty to his belief by accepting imprisonment, a life more rigorous than he would find in the armed services? The fact is that conscientious objectors make their choice in order to fulfill the gospel message: "Love your enemies, do good to those who hate you, bless those who curse you, pray for those who speak evil of you" (Luke 6, Matthew 5).

They have a long tradition within the church to support their stand: Origen, Lactantius, Cyprian, the Council of Nicaea, all the way up to Piux XII and many contemporary theologians, including Cardinal Bea, Father Régamey, Father Yolif, Fathers Lorson and Congar (who call conscientious objection "an exceptional vocation, to bear witness to what is both possible and necessary"), Father de Seras, and Father Daniélou (for whom conscientious objection is "a vocation to sanctity").[24]

There are thirty countries which have abolished, or never adopted, obligatory military service. In addition, there are thirteen countries with obligatory conscription which recognize and regulate conscientious objection. We do not conclude from this that the only teaching of the church is that one must declare oneself an objector. We would simply point out that the order-of-the-day offends by its profound superficiality. Grave and offensive assertions are made without proper grounds. The document utterly ignores the Gospel, tradition, and Catholic theology, not to mention the anguish the church has recently been undergoing in its efforts to resolve this problem. For a group of priests, that amounts to serious negligence.

Their declarations only sharpen and intensify some questions that have been arising lately in public opinion and particularly in Catholic circles. These are questions on which the military chaplains should make known their own thinking.

People are asking: what do the chaplains think about their relationship to the military administration? (Why, for instance, must a chaplain be a lieutenant, a captain, or a colonel?) Do they consider the church to be compromised by practices and attitudes that are clearly not drawn from the gospels? (For example, attendance at mass in full military gear with weapons; indirect or direct pressure to take part, and all that this entails.) Are human values being affirmed, such as personal dignity, freedom of expression, fellowship and love between human beings? Or have discrimination, authoritarianism, and expediency been made into a way of life? What matters more: the rank or the person?

We do not wish to detract from the merits of so many military chaplains, but it seems to us that as an association they have never disclosed their own views on all these issues. On the subject of conscientious objection they have expressed themselves, but they ignore the fact that the objector has offered us a comprehensive reply to all of these questions: a reply of love. None of us has been a conscientious objector, but we count ourselves among those who look with sympathy and even envy at the young men whom a religious and human imperative has led to such a choice.

Those men remind us, among other things, that conscientious objection is but a political response to a problem that is much larger: to reject war effectively, to be real peacemakers, we must bring our weight to bear on the institutions and mental attitudes that make war possible or even inevitable. The choice of the objectors is a prophetic calling, and therefore not one for everybody. But we need them to confront all of us with the Christian and human ideal which compels us to harrow certain political, social, and economic relationships that have made injustice an entrenched reality in our midst, and obliges us to create new structures that allow us to live as humane neighbors: structures guaranteed not by arms, not by threats, not by hot wars or cold wars, but by the message of Good News proclaimed to the poor.

Carlo Bianchi, Bruno Borghi, Enrico Bougleux, Alberto Brunetti, Giorgio Pelagatti, Vittorio Nocentini[25]

———— IV ————

Complaint Filed against Don Lorenzo Milani
by a Group of War Veterans

Milani, Borghi, and their co-signers became the targets of much opposition. This took a most threatening form in a formal complaint filed by a veterans' organization and demanding prosecution. The complaint filed against Don Lorenzo was itself a public statement added to the controversy.

His Excellency
The Procurator of the Republic
Florence

The undersigned war veterans, whose most sacred inheritance — their ideals as citizens and as soldiers — has been deeply and painfully molested, wish to present to Your Excellency the following facts for your considered, impartial, and settled judgment.

Several months back the Court of Cassation,[26] whose mission it is to discern not only the law but also the authentic national conscience, dismissed the appeal of Father Ernesto Balducci against the sentence imposed on him by the Court of Appeal for Florence for his encouragement of so-called "conscientious objectors."[27] That decision won the support of public opinion, especially in veterans' circles.

On the 11th of February, the anniversary of the Reconciliation between the Catholic Church and the State of Italy, the military chaplains of Tuscany unanimously adopted the following order-of-the-day:

> The retired military chaplains in Tuscany, in the spirit of the recent national convention of their association which took place in Naples, offer respectful and brotherly acknowledgment to all of Italy's Fallen. It is their hope that finally, in God's name, there be an end to all differentiation between soldiers of any campaign or any military unit who laid down their lives in sacrifice for the sacred ideal of Fatherland. As for what some call "conscientious objection," the chaplains consider it to be an insult to the Fatherland and to its Fallen, as something alien to the Christian commandment of love, and as an expression of cowardice.

You will observe, Mr. Procurator, that this was a restrained document, direct and to the point, inspired with genuinely Catholic sentiments and with a warm love for Italy. That is the Italy which these men, our priests and our comrades, have humbly served in peace and in war, loyally and courageously standing at our side in the dark moments of danger, and giving comfort to the final, tragic, dying moments of so many Fallen, or even giving up their own lives in the accomplishment of their arduous and noble duty of fidelity and of love.

The order-of-the-day of the chaplains was reported in both the local and the national press. The public thus became abundantly aware of the fact that Florence was the source, not only of voices inciting people to cowardice and to straightforward treason, but also of admonitions to reconciliation, to harmony, and to a sense of duty.

Soon afterwards, unfortunately, not only the military chaplains but all of the parish priests of the diocese and the province received a letter printed and signed by Don Lorenzo Milani, the present priest in charge of Barbiana near Vicchio di Mugello. This came as a shock, but their heartfelt distress was only then beginning.

Milani, apparently not content with having offended and shocked the conscience and the dignity of men he might rightly have considered his brothers in faith and in charity, gave the widest publicity to his document: first by interviews and later by publishing its entire text in the weekly magazine, *Rinascita*, a copy of which is enclosed.

Reading this gives us the impression, as we are sure it will give you also, distinguished Magistrate, that it is an expression of revolt, and yet at the same time one of genuine torment and compassion. It brings to mind the words of our Redeemer: "Forgive them because they know not what they do."

Allow us to extract from context and to highlight a few of the more caustic, harsh, and crudely offensive passages:

Then I must say to you that I have no Fatherland.

If we should find that the history of our army is implicated in offenses against the Fatherlands of others . . . then you ought to explain who defended the Fatherland and its honor more: those who objected or those who by their obedience made our Fatherland odious in the eyes of the entire civilized world?

You should have educated our soldiers for objection rather than for obedience.

It was, to be precise, the brigands who won. Today every one of them has a statue in some Italian piazza commemorating him as a hero of the Fatherland.

The war following 1866 was another war of aggression.

Then we come to 1914. Italy attacks Austria of which, this time, it had been an ally.

Was Battisti a patriot or a deserter?

Those who speak as you now speak also dishonor the church.

To begin with, the Fatherland — we, that is — are paying you or have paid you for that very purpose.

Then, thank God, our Fatherland lost the unjust war which it had unleashed.

And yet you heap injury on a few courageous men who have ended up in prison for doing what St. Peter did.

They have sacrificed themselves for a misunderstood ideal of Fatherland, while trampling underfoot every other noble human ideal.[28]

The publication of this circular letter aroused an indignant and more justified reaction from the Police Association of Florence, whose committee on resolutions met on the evening of the 10th of March and unanimously issued the following order-of-the-day:

Resolved:

That the Association express to the military chaplains of Tuscany its profound gratitude for their order-of-the-day approved on 11th of February, which sets forth nobly the highest principles of loyalty to the eternal love of Fatherland and of just condemnation for the conscientious objectors who give open display of their native cowardice; further,

That it regrets the contemptible attacks directed against these chaplains by a priest in one sector of the press; further,

That it recognizes in such a treacherous attack that sort of irrational extremism which encourages desertion and the defamation of the armed forces; and finally,

That it calls upon competent judicial authorities to direct their attention, as is their duty, to these offenses.

The points which Don Milani sets forth constitute, when taken together, a radical and total condemnation of one century of Italian history. They omit but one brief period of less than two years. The period he pretends to review had its bright and its dark patches, its heroism and sacrifice on either side of the bloody barricade: all of this not to be forgotten, but surely to be subordinated to the need for civil harmony, for mutual respect, and for reverence towards all of the Fallen.

Here is a chronicler who writes in bad faith; his precise objective is to fling mud by the bucketful on what was the passion, the goodwill, the sacrifice of a people's desire to rise from slavery to unity. His purpose is to do harm to the Italian Army, which was such a marvelous protagonist throughout the course of this history. Thus his purpose makes it quite clear that his entire document, and his interpretation of those historic events, must be dismissed as completely false.

Take but one example, that of the Great War, which Milani defines as a war of "aggression against Austria";

on the contrary, it was one futher episode in our national Risorgimento and had as its purpose, surely not to trample another people underfoot, but to liberate our brothers in Friuli, the Dalmatian coast, and the Tridentine mountains — Italians by heritage, by language, by history, by blood — who were eager for the fulfillment of what the divine Poet had foretold:

> As at Pola near Quarnero,
> the palisade of Italy,
> the gulf that bathes its shores.[29]

Our troops — dogged, patient, and admirable — are portrayed instead as naïve, uneducated, incapable of discerning the right path, and "poisoned" by propaganda.

To remain within the borders of uncontested history, we might point out that these same Austro-German enemies had written in their own dispatches the most appreciative commendations of the scrappy little Italian infantryman. How would such heroism be imaginable without a heartfelt determination to fight and to endure for a noble ideal?

For these reasons, Mr. Magistrate, the undersigned believe that the facts and documents set forth here constitute an extreme instance of crime as clearly described in the current dispositions of the Penal Code. They therefore file this formal complaint against the author of the article, Don Lorenzo Milani, and against the editor of the publication *La Rinascita*, with the request that you institute criminal proceedings against them. They file a separate complaint against the signers of the letter published in the same issue of *La Rinascita*, entitled "Conscientious Objection is not Cowardice."

Your Excellency, Mr. Procurator, we are certain that

you will wish, by your actions as Magistrate, to vindicate the right which has been offended. Our criminal complaint is motivated by no spirit of rancor, but by the undying respect in which we hold our duty to the unforgettable Fallen. We who have survived commemorate them when we recall the golden, cautionary verse of a genius of Italian poetry whose ashes rest here in Florence, in the Temple of Holy Cross:

> Blood that was for Fatherland spent
> Mourn and revere with true sentiment.[30]

With profound respect . . .

---- V ----

"The Fatherland and Don Lorenzo"
An Editorial by his Co-defendant,
Luca Pavolini

Among all the editors who received the Milani open letter, the only one who chose to print it was Luca Pavolini, a lifetime activist in the Communist Party. Pavolini had known Milani when both were children (they were only a year apart in age), when their families were acquainted. He came from a Catholic family whose political orientation was both ardent and leftist; this, by his own account, led him naturally to the Communists but also, after the excommunication decree of 1948, meant estrangement from the church. Pavolini had given Rinascita *a high intellectual tone, and had kept readers abreast of other documents that marked the Catholic discussion of warfare and pacifism. Milani made no special claim on their old acquaintance, but had simply put his statement in the mail. Even after it had led to their joint indictment, Pavolini asserts that the two men never met or corresponded. But a lengthy editorial by Pavolini, published during the summer when both were awaiting trial, revealed that he had for some time taken an interest in Milani's controversial career within the church.*

Look what is going to happen, Don Lorenzo: we are going to end up together on the defendant's bench. When

41

we played together as children, that was certainly nothing we could have expected. Nor that you would become priest of a country parish and I the editor of a Communist journal. Since then we have never had the occasion to meet, but I have had plenty of opportunity to know what you were doing and writing. In fact, when your *Esperienze pastorali* appeared, it fell to me to write the review that appeared in *L' Unità*.[31] Today I reread that article. I found it, more than anything else, "sectarian." I appreciated, of course, how much there was in your book that was new and attractive (an anticipation, in fact, of the atmosphere of Pope John!). I underlined the strong and strenuously argued accusations. But in the end I fell out with you because you were a competitor of our Casa del Popolo[32] and because of your rigorous orthodoxy, which seemed to me to be absolutist and backward. On this last matter, it was certainly none of my business to take you to task. That was something the *Osservatore Romano*[33] was to do instead. This is what they had to say:

> The curate of San Donato, in his efforts to gain popularity with the young proletarians of this tiny parish, could imagine no better strategy than to share with them a very rigid and hostile classism, the tactics of struggle used in labor unions and politics, the overthrow of society with its present structure and organization, a systematic contempt for Catholic activists in the social and political fields, and a contempt no less systematic and ruthless for the bourgeoisie, who are persistently described as the number one enemy of the poor.

This was intended to justify the decision by the Holy Office to have *Esperienze pastorali* withdrawn from sale and to forbid its reprinting or translation. It apparently counted for nothing that the imprimatur had been given by Cardinal Elia Della Costa, then the Archbishop of Florence, and that the preface was written by Archbishop Giuseppe D'Avack of Camerino.

Forgive me if I dwell awhile on those events of seven years ago. That classism they accused you of: where did it come from? Your parish of San Donato straddled the mountains of the Mugello and the plains where Sesto Fiorentino and Prato rise out of the ground. You could see with your own eyes

a striking phenomenon, so typical of Italy today: the exodus from the villages and wretched farms of the hills and mountainsides, the unstemmable flow of manpower down towards the potteries of Sesto, the mills of Prato, and the factories of Florence. All the contradictions are there close at hand: out one window you can see the crisis and degradation of agriculture, and from the other you observe the exploitation and the dismissals of industry. From the midst of all this, Don Milani shares his own priestly experiences . . .

One would have to admit that he betrays his classism, for example, in his defense of the right to strike, which Don Lorenzo Milani asserts as the affirmation and means of liberty for the worker. It is there too in his harsh critique of capitalist exploitation and its treatment of employees, especially of the youth. One sees it as well in his condemnation of the favoritism used in hiring, and of the humiliating way in which parish priests have to do the work of government and union officials. It is there when he denounces the enlargement of church property holdings, with the inevitable consequence that priests are confused with landlords. And it inspires his bitter challenge of the way more and more social interests and institutions are taking the church into their compromising embrace, making her the guarantor of the present capitalistic property system.[34]

Those are the things they were not ready to forgive then, Don Lorenzo (those were the days of the Giuffrè scandal);[35] and they are not going to forgive you now either.

I recall that early in '59 the Communist Federation of Florence asked me to take part in a debate about your book in a small village of the Mugello. The auditorium was packed, many of your young people were there, and the discussion was sharp and lively. Then, as well, I was undoubtedly partisan; "too political," they told me. For there was one point where I could not agree with you and your book. With every good reason you were dissatisfied — as I know you still are — with the desperate inadequacies of the Italian school. Masses of young people are being turned loose on society without that minimum of information, and therefore of self-protection, which they need to survive the cunning of a capitalistic civilization and its propaganda. This led you to rail — as I know you still do — against the use of parish centers (and of the People's Houses) as merely recreational facilities in order to attract young people. You argued — as I know you still argue — that the parish centers and the People's Houses ought to sponsor programs of instruction and of culture. That is why you run a school for your boys, with so much sacrifice and success. Now that is all to the good and, granted your view of culture, it is a sound accomplishment. But from my point of view it is both an illusion and a mistake to imagine that one can rectify the miserable failure of public education by a sort of missionary approach to the school. A few people will benefit, but there are millions in need. It is the task of a political party and of a mass movement such as I belong to (though I would say that even priests like you who are employed by the state ought to take the same approach) to press the state and the government to fulfill its own responsibilities. Public education is a social responsibility, a duty of the state, and not anything that ought to be left to the good will of the parish priests. You will produce magnificent results yourself: of that I have no doubt. But as for some of your colleagues . . . about them the less said the better. In any case, on this point we did not agree with your friends, and we all raised our voices a bit. Perhaps you and I can reopen the subject again at the end of October, when we meet in the courtroom of Section Four of the Tribunal of Rome.

Now we have come to a more recent issue, the ruckus over conscientious objection. In the meantime you had been transferred to a still smaller parish, the church of San Andrea in Barbiana, a dependency of Vicchio di Mugello. Every once in a while the glossy magazines have put you in the news, accusing you — among other things — of being intransigent, pugnacious, aggressive, a Savonarola. I suppose you take all that as a compliment. The age of Pope John came and went. Father Balducci was tried and convicted. And one day you read that the retired military chaplains in Tuscany had held a meeting on the anniversary of the Lateran Pact, and had adopted a resolution. The retired chaplains, according to their resolution, consider conscientious objection "to be an insult to the Fatherland and to its Fallen, as something alien to the Christian commandment of love, and as an expression of cowardice."

So you wrote an open letter and had it printed as a broadsheet of two closely argued pages. I don't want to edge our lawyers aside by doing their work, but your letter really had very little in it about conscientious objection. You merely say, near the end: "The human sentence imposed on them is simply that they have disobeyed the law of men, not that they are cowards. Who has authorized you to add insult to that injury?" Period. For the most part you wrote to a larger theme; you gave us a lesson about patriotism.

First you laid down a basic principle.

If you persist in claiming the right to divide the world into Italians and foreigners, then I must say to you that, in your view of things, I have no Fatherland. I would then want the right to divide the world into disinherited and oppressed on one side, and privileged and oppressors on the other. One group is my Fatherland; to me, the others are foreigners. And if, without being disciplined by the church, you have the right to teach that it can be a moral thing—even heroic— for Italians and foreigners to tear each other to pieces, I claim the right to say that then the poor can and should take up arms against the rich. At least in the choice of weapons we enjoy the advantage. The arms which you condone are horrible devices of war to kill, to mutilate, to destroy, to make widows and orphans. The only weapon I condone are noble and bloodless: the strike and the ballot.

Next, you grounded your thinking about the Fatherland on a reexamination of one hundred years of Italian
history: a century during which, sadly, our Fatherland
so often engaged in aggression against other peoples'
Fatherlands. Should we then have obeyed or objected,
you ask. Were those who obeyed and went to fight for
Franco the right ones, or was it the others who "objected"
and took the opposite side? Should we, or should we not,
have objected after the eighth of September?[36]

When your broadside arrived at *Rinascita* we thought
it was an interesting point of view, and we printed it,
just as a few weeks earlier we had printed the letter sent
to the Council by fifteen French worker-priests. All of
this was evidence, we thought, of currents stirring the
Catholic Church despite the official efforts to haul things
back to the way they were before John.

Of course there was a great uproar. All the most in-
competent and Fascist-oriented papers set out to cover
you with reproach: *Specchio, Secolo, Tempo, Nazione.* Some
hysterical statements found their way into print. In one
bold-face, front page piece on 19 March, *Tempo* stated
that in your "dirty booklet" you had uttered "the horrible blasphemies of a man possessed," and that no one
had ever spoken "things that were more perverse, more
insane, more shameful." There were some cowardly hints
that you ought to be roughed up physically, and the
government was even told to remove you from your
parish! A few days later, on the 24th, *Tempo* went on
the attack with an editorial by an accredited Catholic,
Nino Badano. Because you wrote of the poor and the
rich, the oppressed and the privileged, he concluded that
you "had made the choice for Communism." He charged
you with "anti-Franco mania," and extolled Franco "who

liberated Spain from the exterminators of priests and nuns," and Moïse Tshombe as well, whose only concern in the Congo, we are told, is "to save the white missionaries from the hands of the Simbas." And so your calls for peace have become a "source of scandal."

It was in that atmosphere that a group of Florentine "war veterans" filed their criminal complaint against you. That complaint brought on a new wave of insults. Some ex-major addressed himself to you in the pages of *Secolo*: "Job lay on his dunghill, prostrate but obedient under the hand of the Lord. With you it is quite otherwise. You wallow and roll in the pool of muck and filth that threatens to engulf our unfortunate nation, in hopes of spreading its stench still farther." Cheers!

There has however been some response to all this campaign. Not surprisingly, it comes from workers. The internal committee of the Nuovo Pignone has approved a statement, jointly drawn up by both management and employees, in which they say that the testimony of men like Father Balducci and yourself "honors our country far more than any rhetorical exaltation of the Fatherland, and sustains and encourages workers who see in it a clear and courageous affirmation of what motivates their struggle for the full accomplishment of the spirit and letter of the Constitution: principles of civilization, and of the concrete development of persons and of society, with full respect for all Fatherlands, and the absolute renunciation of war as a means for resolving inequities among peoples." "It is urgent and necessary," say the workers at Nuovo Pignone, that "conscientious objection be legally recognized and regulated in Italy." The internal committees of many other large corporations in Florence added their names to this statement: ATAF, ASNU,

TETI, FIVRE, SAITO, Cure Foundries, Italgas, and Romer.

As you know, the prosecutor in Florence forwarded the complaint to his colleague in Rome, since *Rinascita* is printed here. It might simply have been filed and forgotten, but they decided to proceed. And so you have been indicted (and *Rinascita* along with you) for "incitement to the crime of desertion and the crime of military disobedience."

The judicial proceedings will bring up once more the issue so poignantly and publicly raised in the trials of Pietro Pinna, Giuseppe Gozzini, and Father Balducci, just as in the days of the film "Thou Shalt Not Kill," which was made by Autant-Lara and which Mayor Giorgio La Pira "illegally" had shown.

There are now sixteen countries in the world that recognize and in various ways regulate conscientious objection, including the Democratic Republic of Germany. Our Constitution states that military service "is obligatory within the limits and procedures established by law," and thus leaves open such a possibility. There have in fact been three bills introduced in the Chamber of Deputies during this session (besides previous bills that were proposed but never discussed) to legitimate conscientious objection: one sponsored by Socialists, another by Unitary Socialists, and a third by the Christian Democrats.

These proposals all endeavor, though in different ways, to allow some form of civilian service (volunteer work, relief projects, etc.) for those who, for recognized reasons of conscience, refuse to be trained in the bearing of arms. The civilian service would last even longer than the military obligation. All the bills begin from the admission that, whatever one's judgment of the "objectors," we must all cope with a fact. The disquieting fact is that in Italy since 1949 there have been ninety-five prosecutions for fifty accusations of objection, and each objector has received an average of two convictions and sentences up to fifty-five months of imprisonment. There are many citizens in prison today with little prospect of being set free (unless by transfer to asylums for the criminally insane) if they do not renounce their convictions. An objector in Italy today could theoretically suffer twenty-four years of incarceration by repeated prosecutions: from the time of eligiblity for service at twenty-one, until the retirement age of forty-five.

Without touching on the merits of the issue, let me deal for a moment with this problem alone. An article in *Rinascita* had this to say on the problem two months ago: "Unless we enlarge the breadth of our national discussion (as this journal had indeed already tried to do), and of our ideological assumptions, and of possibilities that go beyond conscientious objection to more radical movements that study and advocate non-violence, passive resistance, and absolute pacifism in the past and in our atomic age, the facts will continue to confront us." The article went on to say that the problem of conscientious objection demands "a firm and contemporary reaffirmation of the democratic principle of the citizen-soldier as the basis for all national and democratic armies. This is especially timely when militarists at home and abroad, under the pretext of specialization, are calling for professional armed forces, which are always the seedbeds of authoritarian movements and a pattern for social structures at odds with any sound and lively democracy."

As you see, I am after all discussing the merits of the case, but I do want to underline the problem. And it does seem fair to emphasize how necessary it is to create new laws to deal with it.

Despite all the coarse insults to which you have been exposed, Don Lorenzo, there is reason to hope that your trial will help reopen a serious discussion on this serious problem of our world today.

Luca Pavolini[37]

VI

Letter to the Judges

The formal complaint was filed with the public prosecutor in April, within only a few weeks of the Milani publication, and the trial was set for the following autumn. As the date for his courtroom appearance drew near, Lorenzo's health was worsening. But it may have been an admixture of calculation and of necessity that led him to send a public letter to the Tribunal of Rome which would hear his case, in lieu of his personal presence and testimony. This allowed him to make a more formal and careful statement that extended and deepened his first public declaration.

Barbiana, 18 October 1965

Your Honors:

I am setting down in writing what I would willingly have spoken in the courtroom. It will really not be easy for me to come to Rome because I have been sick now for some time. I am submitting a doctor's certification and I ask that you proceed in my absence.

The illness is the only reason why I am not coming. I wish to make this clear, because since the day that Victor Emmanuel's troops seized Rome, Italian priests have been suspected of having little respect for the state. Indeed, that is the accusation being laid at my door in this trial. But it is an ungrounded reproach against many of my brethren, and in my case it is entirely without foundation. I shall explain to you, in fact, how I have been at pains to impress on my boys a feeling for the law and a respect for the courts of mankind.

Let me offer an explanatory note about the defendant. The things I was trying to say with the letter which led to indictment are of intense meaning to me as a teacher and as a priest. In these two garbs I know how to speak on my own behalf. I therefore requested my attorney not to make a presentation in court. He has however explained to me that this is something he cannot promise, either as a lawyer or as a man. I understand his reasons and I have not insisted.

I offer another observation, with respect to the magazine which stands charged along with me for having offered me the courtesy of its pages. I had distributed on my own initiative the letter with which I am charged, as of the 23rd of February. Only later, on the 6th of March, did *Rinascita* republish it, as did other journals afterwards. Therefore it is a coincidence, a legal technicality, that I find myself as a co-defendant with a Communist magazine. Perhaps if it were on a different issue there would be nothing bizarre in this. But the journal does not deserve the honor of flying colors which do not suit it: ideas like freedom of conscience and non-violence. This situation does little to clarify things, and may mis-educate the young people who are going to be following this trial.

Let me come now to what motivated me to write the letter with which I am charged. But first you may want to know how it is that besides being a parish priest, I am also a teacher.

Mine is a mountain parish. When I arrived there was only an elementary school: five grades in one room. The children left the fifth grade half-illiterate and went out to work. They tended then to think of themselves the way others did: as of little or no account. I decided then that I would spend my life as pastor for their civil betterment, and not only their religious welfare. And so for the past eleven years the greater part of my ministry has consisted in a school.

City people are bewildered by its schedule: twelve hours a day, 365 days a year. Before I arrived, the children kept to that same schedule (and a great deal of fatigue besides) to provide city people with wool and cheese. There was little to be cheerful about. Now that I make them abide by that schedule in school, people say that I am wearing them out.

This might seem to have no bearing on the trial, but it would be difficult for you to understand the drift of my argument if you did not know that the children, for all practical purposes, live with me. We receive visitors together. We read together: books, newspapers, and mail. We write together.

Even if it is a crime, I had the moral obligation to speak out. I had two motives: a motive of the moment, and a motive more profound.

The motive of the moment . . .

We were together, as we always are, when a friend came by with a newspaper clipping. It was entitled "A Communiqué of the retired military chaplains in the Region of Tuscany." Later on we learned that even the attribution was incorrect. Only 20 out of a membership of 120 were present at the meeting. I had no way of knowing how many had received notice of the meeting. Personally I know only one member: Don Vittorio Vacchiano, priest of the chief church in Vicchio. He has informed me that he was not invited to the meeting, and that he is angry at the substance and the form of the communiqué.

The text is, in fact, gratuitously provocative. Think, for instance, of the phrase, "expression of cowardice."

Professor Giorgio Peyrot of the University of Rome is collecting all of the legal decisions handed down against Italian objectors. He tells me that from World War II until now there have not been more than 200. He knows of 186 cases, and has the documents for 100 of them. He assures me that in no single one of them has he found the word "cowardice" or any equivalent. In some, on the contrary, he has found expressions of respect for the moral composure of the accused. For instance: "From the entire behavior of the accused one must conclude that he has fallen into the toils of the law out of love for his faith" (two sentences of the Military Tribunal of Turin: 19 December 1963, defendant Scherillo; 3 June 1964, def. Fiorenza). In three cases the Military Tribunal of Verona recognized the motives of the defendants to be of particular moral and social merit (19 October 1953, def. Valente; 11 January 1957, def. Perotto; 7 May 1957, def. Perotto). I am submitting the complete text of the research results which Professor Peyrot has been good enough to draw up for me.

At any rate, I was sitting there surrounded by the children in my double role as teacher and priest and they looked at me with expressions of disgust and fury. A priest who does injury to a prisoner has always given offense. All the more when the prison is an ideal. I had no need to point that out to my children. They had already sensed it. And they had also intuited that now I was obliged to give them a lesson in life.

I had to teach them how a citizen reacts to injustice. What it means for a citizen to enjoy freedom of speech and of the press. How a Christian reacts when it is a priest or even a bishop that has gone amiss. How each one ought to hold oneself responsible for everyone else.

On one wall of our school we have written in large script: "I Care." It is in English, an untranslatable slogan of decent American youngsters: "It makes a difference to me; I take it to heart." It is the exact contrary of the Fascist slogan: "I couldn't care less."

When the communiqué reached us it was already a week old. So we knew that neither the civil authorities nor the religious authorities had responded.

And so we responded. An austere school like ours, which does not have recreation or holidays, has all kinds of time to think and to study. For that reason it has the right and the duty to say the things that others do not say. It is the only recreation that I allow my children.

So we took down our history books (simple textbooks at the middle school level, not the monographs of specialists) and searched across the span of one hundred years of Italian history in search of a "just war." A war, that is, which would have conformed to Article 11 of the Constitution. It is not our fault that we did not find one.

From that day to this, we have had many disappointments. Dozens of anonymous letters arrived, full of insults or threats, signed with only a swastika or the Fascist symbol. We were misused by some journalists who conducted "interviews" that were dishonest.[38] Then followed incredible conclusions drawn on the strength of those "interviews" by people who never bothered to check their accuracy. We were poorly understood by our own archbishop (Letter to the Clergy, 14 April 1965). And our letter has now become the object of criminal proceedings.

But it was a constant consolation to keep before our eyes those thirty-one Italian young men, convicted conscientious objectors, who are held in the prison of an ideal. They are so different from the youth who crowd the stadiums, the bars, the dance floors, who live to buy themselves machines, who follow the fashions, who read the sports magazines, who are so uninterested in politics and religion.

One of my boys now has as his religion teacher at the Technical Institute the head of those military chaplains who wrote the communiqué. I gather that in class he speaks often about sports. That he tells them how he is an enthusiast for hunting and for judo. That he has an automobile.

He was in no position to call "cowardly, and alien to the Christian commandment of love," those thirty-one youngsters. I want my boys to be more like those he accuses than like him. Yet I do not wish them to end up as anarchists.

The motive more profound . . .

At this point I had better explain the basic problem that every school faces. It brings us to the central issue of this trial, which is why I as a teacher am accused of having committed *apologia*, or advocacy of crime: I stand accused, that is, of running an evil school. We need to be in agreement, therefore, about what a good school is.

A school is different from a courtroom. For you judges what counts is that the law be maintained. A school, by contrast, sits astride the past and the future, and must endeavor to make both of them present. It is a delicate art to lead the children along that razor's edge. We must form in them, on the one hand, a sense of lawfulness (in this our work resembles yours), and arouse in them, on the other hand, a desire for better laws: a political sense, if you will (and in this our work differs from yours).

The tragedy of your profession as judges is that you know you must judge with laws that are still not entirely just.

There are judges still living in Italy who in years past have had to sentence criminals to death. If all of them would be appalled to think of doing such a thing nowadays, we have teachers to thank for having helped us progress, by teaching us to criticize the laws which were then in force.

This is why, in a certain sense, a school lies beyond the reach of your juridical warrant.

A youngster is not yet legally responsible and does not yet enjoy the sovereign rights of an adult. He must prepare to exercise those rights tomorrow, and so in one respect he must obey us and we must answer for him. Yet in another and more salient respect this is so that tomorrow he will frame better laws than we have done. Thus a teacher must, as best he can, play the prophet, and divine the "signs of the times," and inspect the eyes of the children to see the wonderful things that they will discern clearly tomorrow, but which we see only in a blur today.

The teacher too is therefore in one respect beyond the reach of your authority, though at the same time he is at your service. If you condemn the teacher, you are undermining the foundations of the legislative process.

Looking toward tomorrow when they will be sovereign adults, I cannot tell my children that the only way to cherish the law is to obey it. I can only tell them that they ought to hold the laws of mankind in such high honor that they obey them when they are just (that is, when they are the support of the weak). When they see that the laws are unjust (that is, when they support abuses by the strong) they must struggle to see that they are changed.

The official leverage for changing laws is the ballot. The Constitution couples it to the leverage of the strike. But the real power source of these two levers it the power to influence other voters and strikers by word and example. And the time will come when there is no better school than to pay in person for a conscientious objection: that is, to violate a law which one recognizes as evil, and to accept the penalty that is provided. Our letter placed in evidence on the defendant's table serves as a school, for example, as does the witness of those thirty-one young men who are imprisoned at Gaeta. Whoever pays in person gives witness that he wants a better law, that he loves the law more than others do. I cannot imagine how anyone could mistake this for anarchy. Let us pray that God send us many young persons capable of such witness.

I learned this constructive strategy of love for law along with the youngsters when we were reading the *Crito*, Socrates' *Apology*, the life of Our Lord in the four gospels, the autobiography of Gandhi, the letters of the pilot at Hiroshima. These are the lives of men who tragically collided with the rules of their world, not to set them aside but to improve them.

In my own very modest way I have applied this to

my life as a Christian, regarding the laws and the authority of the church. I am a stringently orthodox and disciplined man, yet at the same time one who is passionately attentive to the present and to the future. No one can accuse me of heresy or of being a renegade. Nor of having pursued a grand career: I am forty-two years old and I am the pastor of forty-two souls!

I have already referred to the wonderful youngsters, the best of citizens and the best of Christians. No one of them has grown up as an anarchist. No one of them has grown up as a conformist. Ask them yourselves: they will testify on my behalf.

But was it really a crime? I would appeal to three principles of law: Italy repudiates warfare; even a soldier has a conscience; and corporate responsibility.

Up to this point I have argued that even if the letter entered in evidence had been a crime, it was my moral duty as a teacher to write it all the same. My point was that if you take away my liberty you would be assailing the school's role in legislative progress.

But is it really a criminal document?

The Constituent Assembly requested us to display in our school a copy of the Constitution, "so as to familiarize the new generation with its improved moral and social provisions" (order-of-the-day unanimously passed 11 December 1947).

Italy repudiates warfare . . .

One of these moral and social attainments is Article 11: "Italy repudiates war as an instrument of assault on the freedom of other peoples." You lawyers say that laws apply only to the future, but we streetfolk say that the word "repudiates" is much richer in significance, and embraces both the past and the future. It is an invitation

60

to throw open all the windows . . . and let in fresh air. To throw open to challenge the history that we were taught, and the concept of absolute military obedience as they are teaching it still.

Forgive me if I tarry somewhat on this point, but our letter was a glance back across one hundred years of history viewed in light of the verb "repudiates," and the public prosecutor has construed it as an incitement to disobedience. Obviously it is our moral evaluation of those past wars that will guide us in whether we should or should not obey in the wars of the future.

When we were pupils our teachers — God forgive them — deceived us in a shabby way. They took us to be simpletons, some of them; and yet they were the ones who had been deceived. Others knew that they were misleading us, but they had not got the nerve to tell the truth. Most of them were probably just superficial. But to listen to them, all wars were "for the Fatherland." Let us examine now four sorts of war which were not "for the Fatherland."

Our teachers forgot to draw our notice to one very obvious fact: that armies march to the orders of the dominant class. In Italy previous to 1880, only two percent of the population had the right to vote. Up to 1909, it was seven percent. By 1913, 23 percent of the people had the right to vote, but only half of them knew that or wished to exercise it. From 1922 to 1945 no one received a voter's ticket, but everyone received summonses to three appalling wars.

Today there is universal suffrage *by right*, but the Constitution of 1947 (Article 3) disclosed with disconcerting frankness that the workers had *in fact* been excluded from access to power. Since there has been no move to amend that Article, it is legitimate to think (as I do) that this describes a situation that has yet to be remedied.[39]

It is officially acknowledged, therefore, that the farmers and workers, i.e. the bulk of the Italian people, have never been in power. The army, then, has marched to the orders of only a restricted class of people.

The dividing line is drawn still further. The salary for a military conscript is 93,000 lire a month if he is a son of wealthy parents; 4,500 lire if he comes from a poor family. They do not eat the same mess at the same table, and the sons of the rich have the sons of the poor as their personal servants.

Consequently the army has never, or almost never, represented the Fatherland in its entirety or in its equality.

But in how many past wars were armies really representative of their Fatherland? Perhaps the army that defended France during the revolution. But certainly not Napoleon's army in Russia. The English army, possibly, after Dunkerque. But surely not the English army at Suez. The Russian army at Stalingrad, perhaps. But not, surely, the Russian army in Poland. The Italian army, possibly, at the Piave. But not the Italian army on the 24th of May.[40]

At school I have only the children of farmers and of workers. Electric light was finally installed at Barbiana only two weeks ago, but conscription notices have been assured of delivery to the door as of 1861. I cannot conceal from my boys the fact that their poor fathers endured and inflicted suffering in war to defend the interest of a limited class (in which they had no part), not the interests of the Fatherland.

Even the Fatherland is a creature; that is to say, it

is a lesser thing than God, and to adore it is idolatry. I think that one cannot lay down one's life for anything less than God. But even were we to grant that one could lay down one's life for a good idol (the Fatherland), we certainly could not condone it for an evil idol (the speculation of industrialists).

To lay down one's life for nothing is worse still. Our teachers never told us that in '66 Austria had offered us the Veneto *gratis*. In other words, that all those dead were dead for no purpose. What a monstrous thing to go off to kill and to die for no purpose.

Had they told us fewer lies we would have caught a glimpse of how complex the truth is. We would have glimpsed how that war, like every war, was an amalgam of heroic enthusiasm in some people, of heroic indignation in others, and of criminal irresponsibility in others still.

I say this because some accuse me of a lack of respect for the Fallen. That is simply not true. I do have respect for those unfortunate victims. That is the very reason I would think it offensive to them for me to compliment those who sent them off to die but took care to preserve themselves. I think, for instance, of the king who escaped to Brindisi with Badoglio and a good number of generals, and who in his haste neglected to issue any orders.

Further, my respect for the dead must never make me forget my youngsters who are alive. I do not want them to come to the same tragic end. If someday they should offer their lives in sacrifice I will be proud, but let it be for God and for the poor, not for Signor Savoy or for Herr Krupp.

Think also of the wars to extend our borders beyond the national homeland. There are still Fascists who write me pitiful letters to tell me that I should wash my mouth out with soap before daring to pronounce the holy name of Battisti. Why was it that our teachers presented him to us as a Fascist hero? They forgot to tell us he was a socialist. If he had survived until the 4th of November when the Italians entered the South Tyrol he would have objected. He would never have taken one step beyond Salorno, for the very reason he had protested four years earlier against the presence of the Austrians on our side of Salorno, and was cashiered as a deserter, as I point out in my letter. "We would be repeating an idiocy," he said, "to claim rights over Merano and Bolzano. . . . Certain Italians too easily mix up the Tyrol with the Trentino, and with weak logic want to extend the Italian frontier all the way to the Brenner" (*Scritti politici di Cesare Battisti*, 2:96–97)[41]. Under the Fascists, on the contrary, mystification was scientifically organized: not only in books, but in the countryside as well. The Alto Adige, where not a single Italian soldier ever died, had three fictitious war cemeteries (Colle Isarco, Passo Resia, San Candido) filled with real bodies dug up over in Caporetto.

When I talk of "borders" I mean, as Battisti meant, that frontiers ought to be drawn exactly between one nation and another. They are not intended to enlarge the satisfaction of those costume-Nazis who gun down twenty-year-old border officers.[42]

As for me, I teach my youngsters that frontiers are an obsolete concept. When we were writing our letter which led to this accusation, we saw that our own boundary stakes are always being moved around. And whatever shifts around by the caprice of military fortunes cannot stand as a dogma of faith, either civil or religious.

They presented the Empire to us as a glory for the Fatherland! I was thirteen at the time; it seems as if it were today. I jumped with joy for the Empire. Our teachers neglected to tell us that the Ethiopians were superior to us. We were going to burn down their huts with their women and children inside, while they had done nothing to us.

That was the cowardly school which — wittingly or unwittingly, I cannot say — prepared for us the horrors to follow in three years' time. It prepared millions of obedient soldiers, obedient to the orders of Mussolini. To be more precise, obedient to the orders of Hitler. Fifty million people died.

After having been so crudely mystified by my teachers at the age of thirteen, now that I am a teacher and have thirteen-year-olds whom I love sitting in front of me, would you not want me to feel the obligation — not merely moral (as I said in the first part of my letter) but civic as well — to demystify all things, including the sort of military obedience in which they instructed us then? Prosecute the teachers who are still repeating yesterday's lies, who from that day to this have never had an inquisitive thought. Don't prosecute me.

Even the soldier has a conscience . . .

We wanted to write our letter without the help of a lawyer. But we do have a copy of the legal Codes at school. In the text of Article 40 of the Military Code and in the jurisprudence of Article 50 of the Penal Code we found that a soldier ought not obey when the action commanded is manifestly criminal. One judgment of the Supreme Military Tribunal, for instance, finds a soldier guilty because he obeyed an order to massacre civilians (13 December 1949, def. Strauch). So your own system recognizes that even a soldier has a conscience and requires him to use it when the occasion requires. How could a decimation have even a suspicion of legitimacy, or a reprisal against hostages, or the deportation of the Jews, or torture, or a colonial war?

Or, to take it further, could there be even a minimal appearance of legitimacy in an act forbidden by the international treaties that Italy has signed? Our Archbishop Florit has written that "it is practically impossible for the single individual to evaluate the many complex aspects that govern the morality of the orders he receives" (Letter to the Clergy, 14 April 1965). He certainly cannot be referring to the order that the German nurses received to kill their patients. Nor to the order that Badoglio received and passed on to his soldiers, to aim at hospitals (telegram from Mussolini, 28 March 1936).

Nor to the use of gas. It is useless to close our eyes to the fact that the Italians used gas in Ethiopia. The Geneva Protocol of 17 May 1925, ratified by Italy 3 April 1928, was violated by Italy for the first time on 23 December 1935 at the Tekeze. The *Encyclopedia Brittanica* takes it as an accepted fact. Even Catholic journalists now denounce the fact (Angelo del Boca in *L'Avvenire d'Italia*, 13 May and 15 July 1965). We have read the telegrams from Mussolini to Graziani: "I authorize use gas" (telegram no. 12409, 27 October 1935), and to Badoglio: "I renew authorization use gas whatever kind and whatever scale" (29 March 1936). Haile Selassie has authoritatively and specifically confirmed this (interview in *L'Espresso* 29 September 1965ff).

Those officers and those obedient soldiers who threw the canisters of mustard gas are war criminals, and they have yet to be tried. Instead, I am being tried for having written a letter which many consider noble. (The most appreciated among so many letters of warm support are those from the internal committees of the leading Florentine factories, from the officers and activists of the CISL of Milan and of Florence, and from the Waldensians).[43]

What are the young supposed to conclude about what a crime is? Today the international conventions are included by reference in the Constitution (Article 10). I teach my mountain folk that they should honor the Constitution and the international treaties their Fatherland has signed more than the contrary orders of a general.

I do not take them to be minors incapable of telling whether or not it is licit to burn a baby alive. They are sovereign citizens of reliable judgment, rich in the common sense of the poor. They are immune to certain intellectual perversions which have a way of afflicting the children of the bourgeoisie. I think of those who read D'Annunzio and then brought us Fascism and all its wars.

At Nuremberg and Jerusalem the guilty were men who had obeyed. The whole of mankind is in agreement that they should not have obeyed, because there is a law which is written well enough in their hearts. A large part of the human race calls it a law of God; the others call it a law of Conscience. Those who do not believe in it under either of these names represent only a tiny, sick minority. They are the advocates of blind obedience.

To condemn our letter would be the same as telling young Italian soldiers that they ought not have a conscience, that they should obey like robots, that their crimes will be on the heads of those who ordered them. Instead, they should be told about Claude Eatherly, the pilot at Hiroshima, who dreams every night of women and children burning and melting like candles, and who refuses to take tranquilizers because he does not want to sleep or to forget what he did when he was a "good kid," a "disciplined soldier" (as defined by his superiors), "a poor, irresponsible idiot" (as he defines himself today).[44]

Corporate responsibility . . .

I once studied in moral theology an ancient principle of Roman law that even you accept: the principle of responsibility *in solido*, of corporate responsibility. The public knows it in the form of a proverb: "The one who holds the bag is as much a thief as the one who steals." When two persons commit a crime together, e.g., an assassin and the one who hires him, you hand down a full sentence to prison for them both, and everyone understands that responsibility may not be cut into halves.

A crime like that of Hiroshima required thousands of people sharing direct responsibility: politicians, scientists, technicians, workers, aviators. Every one of them quieted his conscience by telling himself that the total responsibility was divided among them all. Remorse reduced to the third or fourth decimal point won't keep any modern man awake at night.

And so we have come to this absurdity. A cave-man gives someone a blow with his club, knows that he has done wrong, and repents of it. A pilot in the atomic age fills the bomb bay of his plane which will in a short while liquidate 200,000 Japanese, and he does not repent.

If I understand the theorists of obedience and certain German courts correctly, they would have us identify Hitler as the only person responsible for the extermination of six million Jews. But Hitler was irresponsible because he was mad. Therefore that crime never had an author.

There is only one way to extricate ourselves from this macabre word-play. We must have the courage to tell the youngsters that they are all sovereign beings for whom obedience is no longer a virtue, but the subtlest of temptations. We must tell them never to hope they can use obedience as a shield to protect themselves from God or mankind, and that each one of them must feel himself totally responsible for every one else.

If this could be achieved, humanity could be said to have made moral progress in this age which might match, in quality and measure, its technical progress.

My letter stands in the most authentic Catholic tradition. If it is a criminal document, then you must prosecute us all. Let me speak in turn of its history, and its teaching.

Up till now I have spoken as a citizen and a teacher who believes that he has, with his school and with his letter, been of service to the civil community, and that he has committed no crime at all. But let me approach from another angle the possibility that you might consider what I have done as criminal.

Because this indictment has been directed only at me and not at all my brethren, it casts a shadow of doubt on my orthodoxy as a Catholic and as a priest. It would appear that you are condemning the peculiar ideas of a strange cleric. But I am not simply a living part of the church; I am also her minister. Had I been saying things at variance with her teaching, the church would have condemned me. That she has not done so is because my letter sets forth elementary tenets of Christian doctrine that all priests have been teaching for two thousand years now. If I have committed a crime, prosecute us all.

I have pointedly avoided any mention of non-violence. Personally, I subscribe to it. I have tried to educate my youngsters in the same way. Insofar as I was able I guided them in the direction of the labor unions (the only organizations that apply non-violent techniques on a large scale). But non-violence is not yet the official teaching of the entire church. The doctrine of the primacy of conscience over the laws of the state, by contrast, most surely is official. It will be easy for me to demonstrate that in my letter I have spoken as a mainstream Catholic; in fact, often as a conservative one.

Let us look first at my account of Italian military history. The history of Italy up to 1929, as set forth in my letter, is identical with what my seminary professors taught us before that date. We were not radicals. My old parish priest used to tell me that *La Squilla*, the Catholic newspaper in Florence, carried thick black borders because it was still in mourning because of the Risorgimento!

As regards the more modern history, i.e., my judgment on the Fascist wars, it may be that one or another of my brethren harbors some leftover nostalgia, but it is a commonplace that the great majority of priests supports the democratic party which was the principal author of the Constitution (and therefore of that word, "repudiates").

And what of my teaching? The doctrine of the primacy of the law of God over the law of men is shared — indeed, vaunted — throughout the entire church. I do not need to hunt down any modern or recondite theologians to sustain me in that point. Ask any child who is preparing for First Communion: "If your father or mother tells you to do something bad, do you have to obey them? The martyrs disobeyed the laws of the state; was that a good thing or a bad thing?"

There are some who misapply the saying of St. Peter: "Obey your superiors even if they are evil."[45] Really. It makes no difference whether the person giving orders is personally good or evil. He is the one who will have to answer for *his* actions to God.

It makes much difference, however, whether what he commands is good or evil because we are the ones who will have to answer for *our* actions to God. It is not beside the point that Peter was writing those wise recommendations to obedience from the prison where he had been thrown for having solemnly disobeyed.

The Council of Trent is explicit on this question (*Catechism of the Council of Trent* 3, Fourth Commandment, Qu. 16): "If the political authorities command something evil they are to be ignored. In explaining this to the people the parish priest should advise them of the bountiful and appropriate reward reserved in heaven for those who obey this divine precept," i.e., to disobey the state!

Certain Catholics of the far right (possibly the same ones who filed the complaint against me) have admired the recent Exhibition of the Church of Silence. The exhibition consists in a glorification of citizens who for reasons of conscience are rebels against their state. So even these superficial people who are my accusers agree with me. Their only failing is that they recall this eternal commandment when the state is Communist and the victims are Catholics, but forget it in the cases (e.g., Spain) where the state calls itself Catholic and the victims are Communists.

These are disagreeable matters, but I have brought them up to show you that the Catholics who think as I do are lined up on all sides.

We all know that the church honors her martyrs. Not

far from your courthouse she has erected a basilica in honor of the simple fisherman who paid with his life for the breach between his conscience and the prevailing statutes. St. Peter was a "bad citizen." Your predecessors on the Roman bench would not have been all wrong to find him guilty.

They were not intolerant towards religion. They had built temples all over Rome to every kind of god, and assiduously offered sacrifices at every altar. In only one religion did their meticulous dedication to law perceive a mortal danger for their institutions: the religion whose first commandment reads: "I am a jealous God. Thou shalt have no other God besides me." It was inevitable therefore that in those days good Jews and good Christians would appear to be bad citizens.

The laws of the state improved after that. Let me say, with all due respect for the anticlericals, that the progress went foward step by step insofar as those laws were harmonized with the law of God. And so it has become easier every day for us to be recognized as good citizens. But it is only by coincidence and not by inevitability that this is so. Do not be surprised, then, if there are still human laws that we cannot obey. Let us improve them still further, and a day may come when we shall obey them all. I have explained that as a teacher in the civil system I am lending a hand to this work of improvement.

Why do I have faith in human laws? In the brief course of my lifetime I think that our vision has improved. Today we are condemning so many evil things that yesterday we were protecting. Today we are condemning the death penalty, absolutism, monarchy, censorship, colonialism, racism, the inferiority of women, prostitution, child labor. We now recognize strikes, labor unions, and political parties.

All of this represents an irreversible accommodation to God's law. It has come to the point that the two great systems of law are so congruent that normally a good Christian can pass an entire lifetime without ever being obligated to violate a law of the state.

For instance, up until this event I have never been under accusation, and I hope that it will remain true after this trial is over. I wish the same for my patriotic friends. Who knows what grief it would cause them to read all the letters I receive from abroad? From countries which do not have obligatory military service, and from those where conscientious objection is recognized. The people who sent these letters are persuaded they are writing to a country of primitives. Some correspondents asked me how long poor Father Balducci still has to remain in prison.

We were observing, then, that today our two legal systems are almost congruent with one another. There are however some exceptions, a certain number of continuing divergences which call up the ancient commandment of the church that we are to obey God rather than humans. In my letter I enumerated several instances of this. Let me add only one more here.

Let us begin with conscientious objection in the strict sense of the term. Recently I have found support within the church on this very point. The Second Vatican Council invites legislators to have respect (*respicere*) for those who, "either to give witness to Christian meekness, or out of reverence for life, or out of a repugnance for the exercise of any kind of violence, refuse for reasons of conscience either military service or individual acts of savage cruelty in which war might involve them." (Schema 13:101. This is the draft proposed by the commission that reviews all Council proceedings; it is therefore quite likely to be accepted in the final statement.)[46]

The twenty military types in Florence have said that a conscientious objector is a coward. I simply said that he may be a prophet. It appears to me that the bishops are saying a great deal more than I did.

Let us recall three other symptomatic facts:

> In 1918 the seminarians who returned from the war were obliged, if they wished to become priests, to request from the Holy See a dispensation from the canonical irregularities they might have incurred through obeying their officers.
>
> In 1929 the church asked the Italian state to relieve seminarians, priests, and bishops from military service.
>
> Canon 141 forbids clerics to volunteer for military service, and obliges them if conscripted to seek discharge as soon as possible. Whoever refuses is reduced to lay status.[47]

The church, then, regards the entire business of military service as conduct unbecoming a priest. With its bright and its dark patches. The sorts of thing the state honors with medals and monuments.

We must eventually face the most burning problem of the last wars, and of those to come: the killing of civilians. The church has never agreed that it might be morally permissible in war to kill civilians, unless it should happen accidentally in pursuit of a military objective.

At school we read in *Giorno* of an article by the Nobel

Prize winner Max Born (*Bulletin of the Atomic Scientists*, April 1964). He says that in World War I the dead included 5 percent civilians and 95 percent military (one might still claim that the civilians had died "accidentally"). In World War II, it was 48 percent civilians and 52 percent military (one could no longer argue that the civilians had died "accidentally"). In the Korean War, 84 percent civilians and 16 percent military perished (at which point one might claim it was the soldiers who had died by accident).[48]

It is widely known that generals study strategy today with "megadeath" (one million dead) as the unit of measurement. This clearly means that arms are actually *aimed directly* at civilians and that perhaps only the military will be spared.

I am unaware of any theologian who holds that military may aim directly (exclusively, one might now say) at civilians. A Christian, then, in this situation must object, even at the cost of his own life. I would add that in my opinion it follows consistently that in such a war a Christian could not take part even as a cook.

Gandhi had understood this well before there was any talk of atomic arms:

> I draw no distinction between those who wield the weapons of destruction and those who do Red Cross work. Both participate in war and advance its cause. Both are guilty of the crime of war. (*Non-Violence in Peace and War*).[49]

At this point I wonder if it is not merely academic for us to be discussing war in terms that were already obsolete in World War II.

It behooves me then to speak of future war as well,

for in indicting me for advocacy of crime they have explicitly concerned themselves with what our boys might or might not do tomorrow. Yet as regards war that is to come, the inadequacy of terms used in our theology and our legislation becomes even more obvious.

It is well known that the only "defense" possible in an atomic war will be to fire off one's weapons twenty minutes before the "aggressor" does. But in the Italian language "to fire off before" means aggression, not defense.

Imagine then a very virtuous state which in its own "defense" fires off its weapons twenty minutes afterwards. That means, of course, that its submarines would release their missiles, for the homeland would already have been removed from the geography of the earth. But in the Italian language this means vendetta, not defense.

I regret the science fiction quality this argument is taking on, but Kennedy and Khrushchev, the two architects of détente, hurled threats of exactly this sort at one another in public. "We are fully aware of the fact that if this war is unleashed, from the very first hour it will become a thermonuclear and world war. This is perfectly obvious to us" (Letter of Khrushchev to Bertrand Russell, 23 October 1962).[50] We are, therefore, talking about tragically real things.

A defensive war, then, no longer exists. Therefore neither does a "just war": not within the principles of the church and not within those of the Constitution.

Scientists have repeatedly warned us that the survival of the human species is at stake (e.g., Linus Pauling, Nobel laureate for chemistry and for peace). And we are here wondering whether it is licit or not for a soldier to destroy the human species?

I hope with all my heart that you will acquit me. The

idea of playing the hero in prison holds no appeal for me. But I must tell you openly that I will continue to teach my children what I have been teaching them in the past. That is, if an officer gives them the orders of a paranoid they have one duty only: to tie him up tightly and carry him off to a sanatorium.

I hope my fellow priests and teachers of different religions and various schools across the world will teach as I have done. Even then some general may find a poor stooge who obeys and thus we may still not succeed in saving the human race. But that ought not dissuade us from pursuing our duty as teachers. If we cannot save mankind at least we shall save our souls.

Don Lorenzo Milani

VII

The Decision and Opinion of the Tribunal

THE REPUBLIC OF ITALY

In the Name of the Italian People:

The 4th Criminal Division of the Tribunal of Rome
in the persons of

1. Dr. Carlo Adriano Testi, Presiding
2. Dr. Vincenzo Simonelli, Judge (delivering
   the Opinion of the Tribunal)
3. Dr. Brunello Della Penna, Judge

delivered the following
JUDGMENT
on 15 February 1966

. . . it is indisputable that the principal, if not the only purpose of the letter is the problem of conscientious objection, and that this problem has come much to the fore in recent years, feeding debates, polemics, and initiatives of various sorts. The most conspicuous initiative has been the submission of four different bills to legitimate conscientious objection — the last of them quite recently — sponsored by numerous parliamentary deputies belonging to political parties both of the Opposition and (mostly) of the Government. The problem under consideration would in fact most conveniently be resolved, as many deputies and Government officials have stated, only by a legislative provision for conscientious objection. Were Italy to move in that direction, it would find itself following a path already established by the greater number of the countries of the world, which either do not presently have compulsory military service (e.g., England, West Germany, Australia, Canada) and therefore have no occasion for this issue to arise, or do have compulsory military service yet give legal recognition to conscientious objection (e.g., The United States of America, Brazil, Austria, Belgium, The Netherlands, and all of the Scandinavian countries). To gain some idea of the vast portion of the world covered by these two groups of states, let it suffice to observe that their combined populations exceed one billion persons. Countries which, like Italy, have no juridical provision for conscientious objection include a few others in Europe, South Africa, and all states with Communist regimes.[51]

Until the Parliament takes up the various legal proposals mentioned above, citizens will exercise their constitutionally protected right to debate the problem, to ponder all its aspects and implications, and to resolve upon a solution. Nor is that a right to be extended only to an élite of intellectuals or of convinced advocates in cultivated circles, or of professionals in politics or education in their official roles, nor, of course, only to the agencies charged under present regulations with the drafting of laws. It is a right that cannot be limited, as regards the general public, to their power to abrogate laws by referendum (Article 75 of the Constitution), or to their right of petition (Article 50). If we are to read the constitutional precepts closely, it is a right that belongs to whoever wishes to give public utterance to his thinking on the subject, pro or con, with no distinction to be made whether the source or means of expression be public or private, official or non-official, collective or individual (Article 21).

It is precisely the confrontation and contrasts, be they ever so pointed and polemical, of diverse opinions on conscientious objection, that will give birth to the elements of an intelligible formulation and resolution of the problem. There can be no doubt that the very constitutional organs responsible for enacting a fair disposition of the problem stand to benefit from the greater availability of data. They can improve their ability to interpret, as their duties require, the currents of public opinion flowing around this issue, to the extent that the discussion has been broad and free, and insofar as the formation of opinion has been spontaneous and *unshackled by anxiety or hesitation*, and the outcome will be correspondingly improved.

Obviously however there are statutory and criminal limits on the manner in which this acrimonious and topical question is addressed, and in which the grounds for an equitable and authoritative solution are proposed. It is true that the right of a citizen to propound ideas in various forms is so rooted in our Constitution's provisions that any limitation imposed on that right is in tension with a fundamental public right, a basic freedom solemnly recognized by the Constitution. But it is also true that such a liberty does encounter limits that are antecedent to criminal law, because they are sanctioned by the same fundamental charter of the state. And the limits upon that right — insofar as the case at hand is concerned — are crimes committed through the medium of the press, which therefore also control the freedom of the press. That there must be limits is not arbitrary, nor is the notion of limit alien to the nature of a right. Limits are implied in the right, provided that limitations on exercise do not compromise the right in its substance but merely confine it to its proper theater of operation as required by the nature of the right itself (Decision of the Court of Cassation no. 1, 3 July 1956). Restraint of abuses in the exercise of rights that flow from the freedom of the press is, in fact, specifically provided for in the same Article 21 of the Constitution (see also Articles 3, 13, and 32), in order to safeguard religious, judicial, and constitutional interests, as well as those of the family and those protecting the dignity of the person.

In respect of the crime alleged in this case, we observe that the protective duty of the state, as the juridical institution within the national society, to guard against abuses of the freedom of the press is exercised on both constitutional and statutory grounds. It is not incorrect to maintain, as regards this kind of case, that that protective duty is essentially fulfilled by upholding those laws which the state considers essential for the maintenance of peaceful relations between citizens and the state itself, and that included among these laws are those dealing with crime.

Thus Article 414 of the Penal Code punishes anyone who publicly incites others to one or more crimes, or who actively advocates one or more felonies (the latter referring to offenses against the character of the state). No

81

one can in this regard indiscriminately take shelter behind Article 51 of the Penal Code, and allege a right to personal opinion. That provision permits anyone to direct violent criticism at a criminal statute, but it in no way permits one publicly to encourage others to violate the statute, or to encourage others to imitate forbidden and illegal conduct, or in any measure to relieve others of their resistance to such conduct or its author (this is what is meant by the crime of *apologia*, or advocacy of crime).

No law can be permitted to have discretionary limits which entirely frustrate the basic purpose of the law itself. The need, the particular character, and the relevance of limits should be matter for great circumspection in a democratic regime. Still, the claim of any law on affirmative support ought not overwhelm or smother legitimate attempts to attach appropriate discretionary limits to it. In sum, the limitations of Article 21 of the Constitution should not be such as to void the right, or to compromise it to the point of enfeeblement.

The problem here is one of interpretation to be guided, in our opinion, by the principle that norms such as Articles 414 and 415 of the Penal Code derogate from the general criterion of freedom of the press: they are of an altogether exceptional nature and, therefore, subject to strict interpretation. The rule of interpretation to be applied here, as a consequence, should be that which is used for fundamental principles of the Constitution. Thus only those manifestations of thought which orchestrate an attack on our institutions and which promote their subversion through violence ought be fit subject for the application of this criminal statute.

One might object — with reference to the crime of *ap-*

ologia alleged in this trial — that the rule of interpretation as set forth here would lead to an altered definition of that crime, at variance with virtually all jurisprudence and much legal teaching, which saw the crime of *apologia* as a crime of presumptive peril. We believe that the traditional understanding of that crime is not substantially altered. Suffice it to study the explanatory note to the statute which emphasizes that the advocacy which constitutes this crime must not be its own only component. It must also have persuasive capacity sufficient to provoke the danger of further crimes, and therefore to threaten the public order. As part of the tradition rightly holds, criminal *apologia* can correctly be defined as *a manifestation of thought consisting in the advocacy of an act which is criminal, or of its author, with propaganda as its purpose, i.e., with the intention of inciting others to imitate the crime.* Since it involves a criminal activity which threatens the public order, it is substantially nothing more than an indirect form of incitement to crime. Some constitutional scholars would insist that the freedom of expression proclaimed in Article 21 of the fundamental Charter can be curbed by no legislative limits in defense of the public order, except when the expression takes the form of an *immediate* incitement to crime.

It is further to be remembered that the Anglo-Saxon legal tradition — considered to be the most open, civilized, and tolerant in matters of free expression of thought — permits the legislator to prohibit only those manifestations of thought which, in their total context, present *in concreto* a serious possibility of provoking, by their persuasive force, material acts or objects which the state has the right to restrain.

We have before us an explanatory legislative note

of a decidedly general texture, bearing on the crime of advocacy — a document which of itself cannot resolve this issue. It remains for us to understand this provision of law in light of the dictates and direction of the Constitution, harmonizing it with the changing requirements of legal protection for the public order, and also with the freedom to express thought protected under present law. It emerges from such a study that *no advocacy of crime can be established* if the opinion expressed is only a challenge to the moral legitimacy of some criminal statute, prior to consideration of its juridical soundness. Still less when someone does not challenge the basic legitimacy of a law on extrajuridical grounds, but wishes simply to point out certain alleged injustices in the way it is being applied.

In light of these juridical principles we hold that the conduct attributed to Milani (and secondarily to Pavolini) does not integrally constitute the crime proscribed by article 414 of the Penal Code. Licitly, and within the area staked out by the limits of the law, he exercised his right freely to manifest his own thought on a topic of social relevance, to wit, that of conscientious objection. It should immediately be added that this broad freedom of expression had already been of generous benefit to the military chaplains of the region of Tuscany — or, to be more exact — those of their number who had signed the order-of-the-day of 11 February 1965 — when they took a clear and vehement position against conscientious objection in the name of their interpretation of the Christian commandment of love, an interpretation that would leave no room, according to them, for conscientious objection, which would for them represent an insult to the Fatherland and to its Fallen, and an expression of cowardice.

Milani wished to reply to this order-of-the-day with the letter which led to indictment, and a group of priests and of Catholics replied by co-signing another letter, also under consideration in this trial. We hold that the authors of these responses also made lawful use of the same freedom of expression of thought of which the Tuscan military chaplains had availed themselves, and thereby contributed further argumentation to the discussion of the problem of conscientious objection, and public appeal for a legislative resolution.

To appraise this differently would be to deprive the principle of freedom of the press of any effective content while retaining its wording. In the case of conscientious objectors, it would lead to the conclusion that they can be attacked, but never defended: and it would bear not only on the course of conduct they have adopted, and which exposes them to the criminal law, but also on the delicacy and clarity of the problem — a problem that is not only a moral one — which arises so abundantly from it all.

One fundamental quality of the two letters in question here, especially in that of Milani, should be noted. There is a dialectical opposition between his defense and the judgment of the military chaplains on conscientious objectors that was not only negative but injurious. There was a strenuous polemic between two conceptually diverse positions: a polemic which drew Milani, after a while, to go beyond the topic of the objectors into issues both vast and profound, such as the concepts of aggressive war, and of defense, and especially of the proper attitude of a priest towards warfare and the bearing of his apostolate on the needs of the combatants. The military chaplains had issued an apodictic statement about

85

the interpretation of the commandment of love, and they had branded conscientious objectors as cowards. Milani did not restrict himself to a simple denial of either proposition. He saw the need to meet each negative and insulting depiction with a symmetrically positive one, for in his opinion an effective refutation required him to show by a series of arguments how gratuitous and unfounded were the derogatory statements, while at the same time inviting his adversaries to a more attentive consideration of the stand that conscientious objectors are taking, and to a more considerate use of language.

Milani did not wish to meet a counter-accusation of apodictic manner and absolute ideology of thought or expression, such as he had directed towards the military chaplains. And so it was insufficient for the defendant simply to deny what they had asserted, to state that objectors were not cowards and that their conduct was not alien to the Christian commandment of love. It was indispensable that he present the objectors in a completely different light, by countering their description as "cowardly" with the only description which is its exact contrary: "courageous."

Whether the defendant, restricted by the cultural and emotional limitations which his letter displays, was successful is quite another question that in no way diminishes the seriousness of the problem. There can be no doubt that the dialectical strategy to which he was bound, for the reasons given above, had as its outcome a gratuitous and unprovoked attack on the armed forces (as we shall note later), via a supposedly historical review of their comportment during several decades of the recent past, as well as an encomium of conscientious objectors. But it would be simplistic in the extreme, as well as unjust (one thinks of the Roman aphorism: *summum jus summa injuria*) to conclude from this that the defendant has been guilty of advocacy of crime simply because the conscientious objector — as an individual who refuses to don the military uniform — is subject to criminal proceedings and is convicted for the crime of military disobedience.

It is worthy of specific mention that conscientious objection is a mental attitude, the expression of an ideology which, as such, can be shared by citizens who are not subject to military duties (either because they have already fulfilled them or because they enjoy some legal exemption) and which, simply as an ideological expression, is not forbidden by present criminal law. Verbal objection is punished by the state only when its concrete expression is the determined conduct of an objector who is subject to conscription, and who refuses to serve under arms, for which the state then prosecutes him for the crime of military disobedience.

Proceeding directly to an even more crucial point: Milani has praised conscientious objection as an idea, and conscientious objectors as bearers of that idea. He has not approved of the conduct to which it led them and therefore he has not approved of the crime they committed. Their crime is presented as an unavoidable effect of the concrete expression, in the form of military disobedience, of the idea, as a fact which could not help being punished under human law.

In other words, he has not glorified rebellion against the law; he has, instead, enhanced the ideals which lead objectors to prefer prison rather than betray them. It will not be forgotten that the act of advocacy, according to the best interpretation of jurists and jurisprudence, requires a specific object: a crime or a criminal. Of course Milani's letter appears to have in mind the cases of conscientious objectors convicted by military courts in more or less recent times, but it is also the case that the letter is concerned with conscientious objectors in general, and not with convicted individuals. He dealt with conscientious objection in general, examining the principles which he took to support it. In so doing, Milani has passed over individual episodes which placed specific objectors on trial before the military courts, and focused the problem of conscientious objection on the universal level, in the field of ideas.

The letter must be subject to scrutiny in its several parts. But that ought be done in view of its context and spirit, and of the author's intentions, lest one simply break it into disjointed fragments in a determination to find some isolated phrase that smacks of criminal advocacy. If we do evaluate it as a whole, however, that does not prevent us from appraising its segments, which we might roughly identify as three.

In his first section Milani expresses his disappointment at the initiative of the military chaplains, and takes them to task for insulting anyone who thinks differently than they do. It is beyond dispute that in this letter we behold what might best be described as a "professional" polemic between priests about the best way to construe the Christian commandment of love. It hardly needs saying that this is not the sort of dispute into which the Tribunal would wish to intrude, if for no other reason than that it deals with opinions, not facts or acts, and has no bearing on the sort of fact-related crime we are considering in this trial, and is irrelevant to what we must decide here. The Tribunal might only note in passing its observation that the order-of-the-day of the military chaplains — who are, note well, priests first of all — does not seem possessed of the best understanding towards those they consider the victims of error.

The Tribunal would be still less ready to hazard an estimate of the official or even the predominating attitude of the Catholic Church regarding conscientious objection, or to canvass the opinion of this or that theologian or this or that Catholic writer on the concepts of just and unjust war, or on the duty of Christians to oppose laws in conflict with their conscience, or on the prerogative of a good Catholic to refuse military service. The Tribunal understands that, although there is no lack of judgments from impressive and high sources (as, for instance, the attestation of respect for conscientious objectors accepted during a session of the Vatican Council), still there has not appeared from the appropriate organs of the Catholic world any precise and clear policy adopted by the hierarchical church on the issue of conscientious objection. It follows then that the individual Catholic enjoys at least a relative freedom of action: a freedom, of course, as regards ecclesiastical authority.

It is appropriate in this case to underline that Milani, in defending the ideas which underlie conscientious objection, has not claimed to be a spokesman, more or less official, of the church, nor has he pretended to identify his opinions as those of the church itself or of a majority of Catholics or theologians and moralists of that religious allegiance. At least in this respect his position is clearly different from that of any other priest under indictment for inciting others to crime and for advocacy of criminal activity, who wished to present his own views as the official teaching of the church: thus lending them an authority and a persuasive force over the intellect of someone else which, at least in terms of the life that person has chosen, they do not of themselves possess. There would be another difference between that priest and the actual one on trial here. The hypothetical priest presumes to announce, not the mere right, but instead the duty of every Catholic to desert in the event of a war of aggression or a total war, thereby inciting everyone who by religious conviction might be responsive to such an imperative to disobey the laws as they stand, without any concern to reform those laws.

Milani did none of this. On the contrary he has said, *apertis verbis*, that the church has not delivered itself of any opinion to the state, either against the conscientious objectors or against the military chaplains. He has made it abundantly clear that the notions he expresses reflect his own personal convictions, and he has not incited the general citizenry to disobey the present laws by refusing to serve the Fatherland in the armed forces. He has acknowledged the inevitability of criminal conviction for objectors under present legislation. He has proposed as the only remedy for this state of affairs, not rebellion and disobedience elevated into a systematic political stance, but the reform and improvement of the law, to accommodate the ideals of the objectors, for their benefit but also for that of society. Society is presently deprived, as Milani explains it, and will long continue to be deprived of the active contribution by these people (a conviction for military disobedience is repeatable indefinitely throughout the years of military service — from twenty-one to forty-five years of age — and a conscientious objector might theoretically spend as much as twenty-four years in prison). Many of them, as has been recognized by military courts which convicted them of criminal responsibility, are persons of considerable intellectual acumen and of good will, educated and culturally impressive: they claim no exemption from military service as an escape, but ask only to be able to replace it with other services, even longer and more burdensome than what conscripts must ordinarily perform.

Our examination of the first part of Milani's letter leads us to observe that it is here the defendant explains his concept of Fatherland and nation. Milani, who seems never to forget that he is before all and above all a priest, besides being a teacher and a citizen, deals with this concept in a manner closely related to his mission as a minister of God. The Tribunal observes that in scrutinizing and interpreting the letter it takes this "status" of the defendant into account. He has not claimed any right to special treatment for his public behavior before the laws of the state, as if he were a priest who considered himself *legibus absolutus*, like a citizen endowed with general immunities from a positive law. Milani's views are those of a man who, by his spiritual formation and his religious mission, projects common ideas into a much vaster perspective than usual. He has an inner imperative to respect absolute and universal values which transcend political, racial, and ethnic boundaries. Yet it should come as no surprise if he expresses concepts which exceed or indeed in some instances run contrary to more commonly held opinions.

In any case, this first part of the letter contains no expression that could be subject matter for the crime proscribed in article 414 of the Penal Code.

91

Then follows the second part of the document, in which Milani offers an excursus on all of the wars fought by Italy since 1860: all of which, in the defendant's opinion, were wars of aggression. The history of our army, consequently, reads as a chronicle of attacks upon the Fatherlands of other peoples, with the one exception of the war of the partisans. One cannot spare the comment that this section displays the defendant's gravely limited information and especially his flawed approach to historical analysis. It may be that Milani's cultural background is extensive, but his ability to inquire into historical events in search of their causes, and to evaluate them in light of contingent circumstances both foreign and domestic, is modest indeed. This is especially evident in his treatment of the Risorgimento and of World War I, which he has disposed of (the expression is not too harsh) in a few summary judgments in which it is hard to tell what predominates: rhetorical flourish, muddled ideas, or impassioned judgment. Milani's entire disquisition is governed by an almost Manichaean (if it is permitted to apply such a word to a Catholic priest) set of contrasts between Good and Evil, heroes and villains, oppressed and oppressors, disinherited and privileged, obedient and objectors. It is the sort of contraposition which is notoriously unfruitful for the historical analysis of people and events.

Nevertheless — and this is the only crucial point for the present trial and the charges herein argued — Milani has not engaged here in a criminally proscribed activity by representing the Italian military establishment in an unrelievedly negative light. True, his essay is clad in only the outer garments of a historical inquiry, while within it is in fact a polemic tract, a journalistic pamphlet: of third-rate quality even in that genre, by being so one-sided, *parti pris*, and in certain passages, perhaps, even downright seditious. Despite these glaring limitations of content, form, and quality, this portion of the letter moves continuously on the historical-political level, as a sequel to the polemic initiated by the military chaplains' order-of-the-day, and offers a sketch of what he thinks should have been the attitude of these chaplains and of the clergy in general, had they been more faithful to the basic tenets of Christianity, in each one of those instances of war.

There is no ground here for a finding of criminality, at least of the crimes of which Milani here stands accused, even though the Italian Army, towards which the defendant shows himself to foster no respect, emerges from his account as less than noble. In a free country the law cannot establish a single school of historical thought, and deny entry to all contending points of view and analytic methods simply because they violate the accepted canons of historiography and introduce practical and emotional concerns that offend the received scholarship.

It is incumbent upon us to notice, however, because of the apodictic manner in which Milani has asserted his views on one hundred years of history of our army, that there is room for judicial inquiry into whether his allegations — as serious as they are shallow and gratuitous (because not sufficiently or adequately supported by evidence) — might have exceeded the criminal limits set forth in article 290 of the Penal Code (Vilification of the Armed Forces), and whether the passage in which he directs particularly stringent judgments against a foreign head of state might be criminal within the sense of article 297 of the Penal Code (Affronts to the Honor of Foreign Heads of State).

In the third part of the document the polemic against the Tuscan military chaplains resumes, and accuses them among other things of having done an injustice to conscientious objectors by their negative assessment that found no support even in the judgments of the military courts, which did not find those who were convicted to be cowardly.

It must be recalled what we said earlier about Milani's dialectical approach. From his point of view the abrupt and peremptory denunciation by the chaplains obliged the defendant to counter what they said in such a way that he could not help praising the objectors. Here too it behooves us to take note of the overall spirit of the document, and of the author's priestly mission.

With that in mind the Tribunal finds the true sense of the letter to be as follows. According to the defendant a conscientious objector is not treated in the same way as a common criminal, who must pay his debt to society, purely and simply, for having violated the criminal law. He is instead an individual who, though subject to punitive sanctions under the present laws, desires by his conduct not only to stand true to his own highest and most intimate moral and religious convictions, but also to make dramatically clear that there is a problem concerning conscientious objection which urgently requires resolution by the competent authorities. What Milani admires is not defiance of the law *in se* or *per se*, but the capacity for sacrifice shown by the objector in his acceptance of criminal punishment, on the strength of his personal ideological convictions. Milani praises him, not because he has violated the law — to which citizens must surely conform their conduct however the law may at the time read — but because he embodies an idea worthy of respect as a witness to a problem that clamors for legislative attention. The defendant's letter is no indiscriminate encomium of anyone who refuses to obey the law and to perform his military service. His precise argument — which he constantly directs towards a legislative purpose — is a defense of all who pay the personal price of imprisonment, which in peacetime at least is much more burdensome than the most rigorous military service, because they think it right to give the duties of their own conscience precedence over one particular duty incumbent upon them as citizens.

One immediately anticipates an objection: surely this is subversive of the very principle of legality and of constitutional government. What would be the effect of conscientious objection on the defense of the Fatherland in wartime and, in general, on the duty of obedience to the laws of the state?

To allay such fears, let us take note of the very modest incidence of conscientious objection in countries which grant it legal acceptance. The Tribunal finds, however, that even on the level of abstract principle this misgiving is unfounded.

At the beginning of his admirable summation, the Procurator argued that the so-called right to resistance is nowhere granted by our present Constitution, and that norms are provided to cover the possibility that Italy could be engaged in an unjust war (Articles 11 and 78 of the Constitution). Without wishing to discuss these assertions in detail, we must at least observe that the confidence which the Procurator places in the power of law even through periods of constitutional crisis is not confirmed by the recent experiences of our country. It proved possible for the natively liberal stock of the Albertine Code to have grafted onto it, without any modification in the Constitution, an authoritarian regime, against which the most honest thing for the Italian people then was to collaborate as little as possible, if not indeed to resist.[52]

In any case it is the very states which enjoy the most stable democratic traditions that have made room for conscientious objection. One ought not imagine that this is explained by the democratic and pacifist character of their traditions, which would render it less possible for one to refuse military service there for authentically ideological reasons. There is indeed a problem within our tradition, one mentioned by the Procurator and of concern in legislative circles, which must be faced before any decision whether and to what extent to allow conscientious objection, since Article 52 of the Constitution declares that military service is obligatory within the limits and procedures established by law. In this courtroom our concern is only to judge whether Milani, by defending conscientious objectors, has committed *apologia*, or advocacy of crime: in other words, whether or not he has exceeded the limits which constitutional law imposes even on the free expression of thought. And the Tribunal finds that this has not been established.

In addition, the statute cannot be said to have been compromised, nor the public order threatened (that is the juridical concern of article 414 of the Penal Code) just because there is someone who takes the side of conscientious objectors. Some of the more insistent opponents of conscientious objection give voice to a fear that were it to become legal in Italy, the obligation to serve the country would collapse. This danger does not exist.

Even if it did, that should not stand in the way of anyone's lobbying for a new law, a law acknowledged to be of civic value and inspired by high ideals (a point that people will never grasp if all they consider is how it might be abused and ignored). More importantly, the abuse they worry about can be avoided by the sensible ability to tell the difference, in time of peace and in time of war, between an individual coward, rebel, or misfit, and someone who makes a conscientious choice, as is his inalienable right, between various forms of service to the Fatherland.

Returning to the Milani letter, the Tribunal finds in it no statements subversive of the constitutional system or dangerous to the public order. It rekindles an ancient concern with regard to compulsory conscription, a concern which has been reformulated since World War II, by inviting people to contemplate an organized violence that takes on apocalyptic proportions. Against that background the defendant views conscientious objection as a witness to a profound conviction against violence and not at all an embodiment of cowardice, antisocial alienation, or defeatism.

Milani's appeal echoes clearly the arguments put forward in support of the bill on conscientious objection before the Parliament. Indeed, his way of putting the issue is sometimes more vibrant and positive than what some of its more celebrated exponents have offered in their official speeches. What he is saying resonates with the publicly presented ideas of noted and esteemed figures in the international community. The Tribunal does not find that Milani has written, in his modest style of limited form and content, words that are substantially different or more rigorous than those of the leading authorities, words that would deserve the accusation that they advocate crime.

Milani's view of the matter is straightforward, and from this angle he has described conscientious objectors as "prophets," insofar as they are precursors, in his opinion, of a day when their position will very likely be reconsidered and given timely legal recognition.

The defendant does not appear to have presented conscientious objectors in such a light as to rally others to follow their chosen line of conduct. His presentation is aimed more at changing the attitudes of those in a position to alter their present legal status. Thus Milani (as also the unidentified authors of the supporting letter entitled "Conscientious Objection is Not Cowardice") has not incited others to disrespect or disobedience or, worse, to revolt against the law as it now stands. He has argued that the law requires amendment, a stance that is morally consistent with sincere and intelligent observance of law as the consistent standard of any liberal regime.

No truly democratic regime need fear the free expression of ideas, however polemic and prejudiced those ideas may seem. It is the unfortunate privilege of the so-called "strong" (meaning authoritarian) regimes that they repress ideas as criminal. To convict Milani for having written on conscientious objection would amount to incriminating, not an action concretely in defiance of a criminal statute, but a simple opinion, insofar as it could be, or might be construed to be, subversive.

The defendant's activity may instead be explained as part of a movement to abolish or to reform a law that in this respect is considered unfair or injurious. In a liberal state like ours this is to be viewed as an exercise of the power to criticize legislation and to participate in the improvement of the social order. It is not to be viewed as a damage or danger to the public interest.

Milani is therefore acquitted of the crime of which he stood accused because the facts of this case do not constitute a crime liable to punishment.

VIII

The Decision and Opinion of the Court of Appeal

THE REPUBLIC OF ITALY

In the Name of the Italian People

The Second Section of the Court of Appeal of Rome, composed of:

1. Dr. Giuseppe Mistretta, Presiding
2. Dr. Nicola Palma, Associate
3. Dr. Tancredi Milanese, Associate
4. Dr. Achille Gallucci, Associate, delivering the Opinion of the Court
5. Dr. Leonardo Murante, Associate

delivered the following
JUDGMENT
on 28 October 1967

. . . The Opinion of the trial judges is undoubtedly a valuable monograph on the points which, though they lie well beyond the field of positive law, the Tribunal chose to consider: questions *de jure condendo*, of religion, of politics, of sociology and philosophy. These same questions have been brought before us again in oral arguments, but they will be left aside by the Court because they do not bear on the decision properly defined, or because they do so only incidentally by their indirect connection with questions of law.

The questions of law were also adequately treated by the first judges, who set forth their premises with exactitude, in full agreement with the principles generally derived from both jurisprudence and doctrine. From their exact examination of law they have derived, however, an inexact solution, which has the effect of denying the juridical principles they had so carefully explained. Therefore, in response to the request of the Ministry of Justice, the judgment of the trial court is revised . . .

If we hold that *apologia* is a manifestation of thought intended to praise or advocate one or more actions designated by the law as crimes, such that the advocacy amounts to an indirect incitement to crime; and if we hold as well that the specific object of such legal protection is the general public order which has been threatened by propaganda on behalf of crime: then the first fault in logical and juridical reasoning to be found in the judgment under appeal today occurs in the passage which states that the document we are judging, though it extols conscientious objectors, does not extol the consequences to which that idea has pointed them. On the contrary, we must make it clear that Milani was not praising the supporters of non-violence, peace, and universal brotherhood; he praised those who had broken the law, and that amounts to praise for the crime, because the two concepts are indissolubly joined. If you praise thieves you are implicitly praising the crime of theft.

Another breakdown in logical and juridical reasoning is found in the passage which states that the publication should be studied as a whole, "in view of its context and spirit, and of the author's intentions, lest one simply break it into disjointed fragments in a determination to find some isolated phrase that smacks of criminal advocacy." Several remarks are in order here. First, the Tribunal might well have acknowledged the symptomatic importance of certain phrases. Second, as we shall shortly see, the Tribunal's reasoning is undone elsewhere by its own confusion between the concepts of deceit and of purpose. But even were we to grant the reasoning of the Tribunal, the Court must observe that it is the overall polemic thrust of the publication which, as the overall context of particular passages, brings one to conclude that its purpose is not to defend an idea and then to urge the need for a change in legislation regarding the obligation of military service, but to extol and praise those whom "many admire"; who "objected," and "defended the Fatherland and its honor more" than those who fought; "courageous men who have ended up in prison for doing what St. Peter did"; "prophets, whose place admittedly is in prison, but it is not very becoming to take sides with whoever put them there"; men who are "not to blame if in Italy they have no choice but to serve their Fatherland idly in prison"; "if we do not wish to honor their suffering," we should at least keep quiet.

The Tribunal offers no in-depth examination of these passages, which offer such unambiguous praise for those who had already violated the law of the state. Nor has it suggested what stronger expressions than these could finally have persuaded them that this is indeed a statement of advocacy for deserters, draft-dodgers, and those men who have refused to obey military orders.

When the quoted passages are placed alongside the entire context of the publication, one sees that it is not these passages which follow from the dissertation (which the Tribunal has already held, under another aspect, to be violative of the law forbidding vilification of the armed forces), but the entire dissertation which follows from these passages, in that it only serves to enhance the praise given the achievements of conscientious objectors by proffering a justifying evaluation of the history of Italy so destructively seditious (all the wars engaged in by Italy during the previous one hundred years, except for the war of the partisans, would have been wars of aggression) that the motive of its author and his purposes in publishing it become altogether apparent. The essay was not intended to treat of the idea of conscientious objection, considered in and by itself. It was designed to create the danger that individuals of scant culture, not gifted with critical judgment sufficient to detect the insidious dialectic hidden in this document, could repeat the criminal actions performed by conscientious objectors who are portrayed in the glorious light of martyrdom, and virtually exalted to the same honors as Saint Peter himself.

The Tribunal has noted the "glaring limitations of content, form, and quality" in its Opinion now under appeal, but did not pursue its scrutiny further into the central teaching which the content and form were meant to serve. Instead, it excused its seditious character by its historical improvisation, by the jumbling together of ideas, by the passionate thrust of polemic which it ascribed to the order-of-the-day of the military chaplains and which it saw as justified by Milani's profound ethical motives.

On the contrary, whenever the juridical good to be protected by the criminal law is injured, this Court will not concern itself with plausible motives of ethics or philosophy or even theology which might have led to a manifestation of thought. Ethical principles never possess an absolute value, because they can be sacrificed to outcomes considered to be more important, such as "the fulfillment of the indispensable duties of political, economic, and social solidarity" (Article 2 of the Constitution), which duties include those of military service and of participation in war to defend the independence of the Fatherland. Lawful regulations cannot be put in jeopardy by principles of any sort which stand opposed to the law. Further, the psychological aspect of crime is to be identified as the *voluntas sceleris*, the decision to perform the forbidden act, and is utterly distinct from the *causa sceleris*, or whatever may have brought about that decision. It is therefore beside the point to lecture this Court about the predominant opinions of theologians, or about proposals for new laws regarding conscientious objection that may be under parliamentary consideration. The only thing that can matter for a judge is the positive law which unconditionally imposes the obligation of military service, with certain specifically noted exceptions. "Tribunals ought not occupy themselves with ideologies, for they are called to judge concrete facts" (Court of Cassation, 1 June 1964, *G.P.* 1964 II, col. 737).

In order to determine the existence of the crime of advocacy, or *apologia*, one must necessarily prescind from inquiry into the substantial validity or the rational or moral grounds of any doctrine which does not bear on principles of law. This is especially true of the teaching set forth in the incriminated publication which, impelled by a seditious and divisive intent, appears to be deeply rooted in those precepts of the gospel which apply only to individuals and not to collectivities. These precepts have been used to prevent social disintegration; still one must remember that the fathers of the church generally accepted the just war despite the generic command to respect the physical life of one's neighbor, because Catholic morality had not abolished the natural law nor suppressed the fundamental rights of the person. It is a dictate of nature, and therefore an inalienable right of man, to defend his own existence and the integrity of his own body against any unjust aggressor.

The Court enters these remakrs because of the need to show that the use of St. Peter's question ("Is it God or men that we ought to obey?") is intended to reinforce the author's intention of extolling conscientious objectors. It effectively increases the danger of violating the good which the law is meant to protect, by giving the impression that conscientious objection, which has been clearly shown to be in violation of principles sanctioned by the Constitution and by norms of law, draws its justification from ethical-religious grounds. In a profoundly Catholic country, such rhetoric is exceedingly suggestive and dangerous, in view of the religious and moral authority attributed to the teaching of a priest like the author of this document.

There is merit in the observation that once the military chaplains had described conscientious objectors as cowardly, it became polemically necessary to rebut this pejorative expression with such as we find in the document: one must either accept the designation of objectors as cowards or refute it, according to one's point of view. But even in open polemics one may not exceed the bounds defined by Article 414 of the Penal Code, for in these matters there is no truth in the maxim that the end justifies the means. It ought to be emphasized, in fact, that the dispute with the military chaplains was an opportunity that was welcomed and exploited, not merely to discuss serenely and objectively the question of conscientious objection as a simple opinion, or its legitimacy as a moral and juridical question — as the Ministry of Justice has rightly pointed out — but by maliciously enlarging the boundaries of the discussion to heap praise and admiration not on the idea and its theoretical supporters, as has been argued by both the Tribunal and by the counsel for the defense in these proceedings with argumentation that is logically and juridically frail, but on the very criminal actions committed by those who "objected" in time of war (deserters) and by those who refused to serve in time of peace. They have been portrayed as defenders of their Fatherland's honor more worthy than those others who, by fighting, "unwittingly trampled underfoot every other human ideal," paying personally for their courageous behavior; we are permitted to "respect their suffering," but asked to abstain from admiring them as many others have done.

All this under the mantle of ethical and religious principles, constructing arguments that invite every citizen to conduct a personal audit of the justice of every war, something that could only plunge us all into anarchy and chaos. It also ignores the fact that it is not military service which is the provocation of wars, but the possibility of war that obliges every man in every nation to offer

himself for training so that he can be ready to fight whenever he is summoned by orders that enjoy an absolute
presumption of legitimacy. The duty of assessing the
legitimacy of a war will be assigned to history, in the
future, and not to the ephemeral ideas and passions of
the individual, in the present moment.

The tract in question has displayed its unilateral character by referring exclusively to the wars engaged in by
Italy. A document governed by realism and objectivity
would have inculcated non-violence in citizens of every
nation, not merely those of Italy. The underlying rhetorical purpose is a simple one: not to defend a utopian
principle of universal peace, but to praise the crime
of military disobedience and desertion committed by
Italians.

One must conclude that this document has inflicted
damage upon the public order, and that it is in the interest of the state to repress any activity which has been
found to subvert the people's readiness to observe the law.

*The Court of Appeal reversed the decision of the Tribunal.
Since Don Lorenzo had died several months earlier while the case
was still on appeal, his name was removed as a defendant before
judgment was rendered, with the explanation that "a crime disap-
pears with the death of the criminal." Luca Pavolini was found
guilty by dint of negligence rather than active connivance, and
was sentenced to the lightest possible penalty: five months and
ten days of imprisonment. The sentence was suspended for five
years. It was quashed little more than a year later, in an amnesty
granted by the highest bench, the Court of Cassation. Today
Pavolini is active as a member of the central committee of the Italian
Communist Party.*

IX

The Laws That Were to Follow

Later in the year that Don Lorenzo has been acquitted, after the public prosecutor had filed an appeal but before the appellate court had reviewed the verdict, the Italian Parliament enacted a new law on this subject.

Law of 8 November 1966, no. 1033:

The Chamber of Deputies and the Senate of the Republic having approved, the President of the Republic promulgates the following law:

Art. 1. The Minister of Defense has the authority, in peacetime, to waive military service for those subject to conscription who possess special qualifications and ask to engage in work for at least two years in a developing country outside Europe.

Art. 2. Work which fulfills this provision must be either in a program of technical assistance rendered through bilateral agreement between the Italian State and the host country, or through institutions or international entities recognized by the Italian State. . . .

Lest this opportunity for alternative service be too widely exploited, it was modified by presidential decree less than a fort-

night after the appellate court had found Luca Pavolini of La Rinascita *guilty.*

Decree of the President of the Republic of 8 November 1967, no. 1322:

The President of the Republic . . . decrees:

Art. 1. The waiver of military service permitted by the Law of 8 November 1966, no. 1033 (1), can be requested by young men subject to conscription who possess the doctorate, or a diploma from a university or technical or teachers' training college, or a qualifying diploma issued by any professional school governed or recognized by the state, or a certificate of enrollment in courses financed or authorized by the Ministry of Labor and Social Welfare, accredited for training and professional formation.

Art. 2. The Ministry of Defense may grant, according to the terms set forth above, no more than one hundred waivers of military service each year. . . .

In the next several years this provision was extended somewhat to allow alternative service in aid of various Italian areas stricken by disaster.

Law of 30 November 1970, no. 953:

The Chamber of Deputies and the Senate of the Republic having approved, the President of the Republic promulgates the following law:

109

Art. 1. Young men whose names are inscribed in the conscription lists from the communes in the valley of Belice (whose inhabitants have been authorized to move either completely or partially because of the earthquakes in January 1968) and who are due to be called up for military service in 1971, 1972, or 1973, qualify on request for a waiver of that service provided they accept employment in a civilian project, of at least the same duration, for the reconstruction and development of the valley.

This alternative is also available to young men whose names are inscribed in the lists from the commune of Roccaforte . . .[53]

Law of 20 December 1971, no. 1155:

The Chamber of Deputies and the Senate of the Republic having approved, the President of the Republic promulgates the following law:

Art 1. The young men whose names are inscribed in the conscription lists for the communes of Tuscania and of Arlena di Castro in the Province of Viterbo, stricken by earthquake on February 1971, and who are due to be called up for military service in 1971, 1972, or 1973, qualify on request for a waiver of that military service provided they accept employment in a civilian project, of at least the same duration, for the reconstruction and development of these communes. . . .[54]

In the meantime, a variety of bills had been introduced in both houses of the Parliament to give legal recognition to conscientious objection.[55]

110

Attention was being drawn to foundational documents that imposed on the Italian people a reconsideration of their law of conscription:

The Constitution of Italy

The Republic recognizes and guarantees the inviolable rights of man, both as an individual and as a member of the social groups in which his personality finds expression, and imposes the performance of unalterable duties of a political, economic, and social nature (Article 2).

The Universal Declaration of Human Rights:[56]

Everyone has the right to freedom of thought, conscience, and religion; this right includes freedom to change his religion or belief, and freedom, either alone or in community with others, and in public or private, to manifest his religion or belief in teaching, practice, worship, and observance (Article 18).

The European Convention for the Protection of Human Rights and Fundamental Freedoms:[57]

1. Everyone has the right to freedom of thought, conscience, and religion; this right includes freedom to change his religion or belief and freedom, either alone or in community with others and in public or private, to manifest his religion or belief, in worship, teaching, practice, and observance.

111

2. Freedom to manifest one's religion or beliefs shall be subject only to such limitations as are prescribed by law and are necessary in a democratic society in the interests of public safety, for the protection of public order, health, or morals, or for the protection of the rights and freedoms of others (Article 9).

The Italian Penal Code:

The exercise of a right or the fulfillment of a duty imposed by the law or a legal order of public authority is exempt from punishment.

If a criminal act is performed by order of authority, the public official who issued the order answers for the crime.

Whoever carries out that order also answers for the crime unless, through error of fact, he had thought he was obeying a legal order.

Whoever carries out an illegal order is not punishable if the law does not allow him access to verify the legitimacy of the order. (Article 51)

The following circumstances shall extenuate an offense . . . :

(1) having acted for motives of particular moral or social value . . . (Article 62)

Pressure was being applied through the courts themselves, where a succession of young men underwent prosecution and appeal for their refusal to answer the call to military service. By the late 1960s the Supreme Military Tribunal noted a discernible swing in public opinion regarding conscientious objection.[58] *Defendants were appealing to the provision in the Penal Code (Article 62), arguing that their refusal to bear arms was grounded precisely on "motives of particular moral or social value." The courts martial steadfastly refused them this as a legal defense. It was interpreted to serve as a lawful excuse only for a conscript to be delinquent in appearing after he was called up. As the courts read the law, a conscript might have been delayed by an understandably urgent, conflicting duty, such as the need to bring in the harvest and save his family from bankruptcy. But an outright refusal to serve at all was something different. Since the Constitution declared military service to be an absolute duty, to allow exemption for individual motives would for all practical purposes invalidate the duty of solidarity with the nation by subjecting it to every citizen's private discretion or whim.*[59]

Finally a law was passed accepting, in a limited way, the principle of conscientious objection.

Law of 15 December 1972, no. 772:

The Chamber of Deputies and the Senate of the Republic having approved, the President of the Republic promulgates the following law:

Art. 1. Those who are subject to conscription, and who declare themselves to be opposed, for indispensable reasons of conscience, to any personal use of arms, can be permitted to fulfill the obligation of military service in ways prescribed by this law.

The reasons of conscience adopted ought to involve a general conception of life grounded upon profound religious or philosophical or moral convictions espoused by the person concerned.

No one may avail himself of this law, however, who at the time of his request holds a license or other authorization to use firearms . . .

Art. 3. The Minister of Defense shall by decree accept or reject the request, upon advice from a commission regarding the soundness and sincerity of the motives espoused by the petitioner. The Minister must decide upon the request within six months, during which time induction into the armed forces is delayed.

Art. 4. This commission is named by the Minister of Defense and includes:

a judge from the Court of Cassation, chosen by the High Judicial Council, as president;

a general or admiral, chosen by the Minister of Defense;

a university professor competent in ethics, chosen by the Minister for Public Instruction;

an assistant attorney general, chosen by the Prime Minister upon advice from the Attorney General;

a psychologist chosen by the Prime Minister. . . .

Art. 5. Young men who benefit by this law must serve either in the armed forces in a non-armed capacity, or in alternative civilian service, for eight months longer than their term of military service would have been had they been conscripted.[60]

Months later the judiciary gave benefit of this new statute to a young man who had not at first expected it. The Supreme Military Tribunal said:

The crime of failure to answer a conscription call, of which [the appellant] Bellassai is accused, occurred before the new law took effect. It was a law that revealed a change in our social and cultural perspective. In a democratic state the law normally acquiesces in judgments that have emerged from the maturing thought of the community, for society sets its mind on certain values even before they find expression in legislation. Thus it can anticipate and promote their legal development.[61]

Don Lorenzo had written to his judges: "A teacher must, as best he can, play the prophet, and divine the 'signs of the times,' and inspect the eyes of the children to see the wonderful things that they will discern clearly tomorrow, but which we see only in a blur today."

This change, in the justice of Italy, came four years after the verdict of guilt had been passed on Don Lorenzo's letter, and five years after his death. He was a man worthy of special remembrance, for he had most eloquently anticipated and promoted the maturing thought of the social community. He abided by the law. He enacted the law as well.

Notes

1. *Lettere di Don Lorenzo Milani*, ed. Michele Gesualdi (Milan: Mondadori, 1970), pp. 172–73.

2. For further biography, see Giorgio Pecorini, *A messa coi carabinieri* (Vicenza: La Locusta, 1968); Antonio Greppi, *Tre racconti di Natale* (Vicenza: La Locusta, 1969); Nazareno Fabbretti, *Don Mazzolari, Don Milani: i disobbedienti* (Milan: Bompiani, 1973); Neera Fallaci, *Dalla parte dell'ultimo: vita del prete Lorenzo Milani* (Milan: Milano, 1974).

3. *La Nazione*, 12 February 1965.

4. "Diseredatati e oppressori," *La Rinascita* (Rome), 6 March 1965, pp. 27–28.

5. The Article continues: ". . . and as a means for settling international controversies."

6. The volunteer army of Garibaldi, acting on behalf of Victor Emmanuel I, of the House of Savoy, King of Piedmont, completed his subjugation of the Bourbon Kingdom of the Two Sicilies by taking Naples. It was, up to that time, the largest territorial acquisition for Piedmont and for an eventually amalgamated Italy.

7. Here Milani is citing some of the remainder of Article 11 of the Constitution, which was to provide for eventualities such as the United Nations, the World Court, and the European Community. The entire Article reads as follows:

"Italy repudiates war as an instrument of aggression against the liberties of other peoples and as a means for settling international controversies; it agrees, on conditions of equality with other states, to such limitation of sovereignty as may be necessary for a system calculated to ensure peace and justice between nations; it promotes and encourages international organizations having such ends in view."

8. Before the third war of Italian unification, Italy signed a mutual aggression treaty with Bismarck's Prussia, the object being to seize the Veneto from Austria. Austria then offered through France to cede the Veneto if Italy would forgo the war. Italy, under General La Marmora, prime minister, refused the offer, with the hope of acquiring Trieste and the Trentino as well. The war proved to be a disaster for Italy. Austria kept Trieste and the Trentino, and ceded the Veneto (whose population failed to rise in Italy's behalf but who, after occupation by the Italian forces, accepted the cession by plebiscite).

9. This was the war against the Papal State to annex the remaining part of central Italy still under the Pope. France, which withdrew its troops from the protection of Rome, had been assured Italy would stand by the Convention of 1864, and that Rome was by international law inviolable. After a staged uprising failed to transpire, the Italian army seized Rome in 1870 and annexed the State.

10. National embarrassment abroad and agitation by socialist groups led to popular outcry for social reform. Mob rule and rampage occurred in Rome, Parma, Florence, and other cities. In Milan, after rioting led to the deaths of two policemen, General Fiorenzo Bava-Beccaris mistook a soup-line of beggars for rioters and turned cannon and grapeshot on them, killing eighty people and igniting four more days of street fighting. These events of May were on questionable evidence explained as a plot by socialist leaders who were, along with radicals and republicans, imprisoned. The universities of central Italy, the labor unions, the newspapers, the small banks, and about three thousand Catholic social organizations were shut down. Railway employees and civil servants were conscripted into the army so as to be under martial discipline and courts. The General's decoration was, to be exact, the Grand Cross of the Military Order of Savoy.

11. In order to take her place alongside other European imperialist powers, Italy created a colony, Eritrea, on the coast of the Red Sea, by sending a military expedition and bribing a local chief-

tain. When the forces moved further inland into Abyssinia/Ethiopia, resistance followed, and a war ensued without any parliamentary oversight from Italy. Though costly in lire and lives, and offering no substantial economic advantage in Ethiopia, the war was continued in order to save face, to provide political success for an unstable government, and to strengthen the morale of the army (the only bulwark against lower-class unrest). Italy was defeated. Six thousand Italian soldiers lost their lives in the last battle — more Fallen in one day than in all the wars of the *Risorgimento* put together.

Fascist desire for an overseas empire led Mussolini to claim Abyssinia in order to propagate a virile race over the face of the earth, as he said. Peasant families were prevailed upon to follow the army as colonists: first into Libya and then into Ethiopia. British and French governments supported the Italian expansion in its early stages. After Addis Ababa had fallen, Mussolini expressed disappointment that only 1,537 Italians had been killed, for this meant that the army had been inadequately blooded and toughened. His son Vittorio published an account of the pleasure afforded by bombing village horsemen, who when hit would liquefy like a budding rose. Gas was used both during the invasion and during later uprisings. Ethiopia ended up costing ten times what it would return economically.

12. Giovanni Giolitti, who was to serve as prime minister in four governments between 1892 and 1921, eventually yielded to right-wing pressure for national expansion and manifest destiny and, having unsuccessfully sent a military mission to China in 1899–1900, he initiated a Libyan war in 1911–12. He was opposed by the Turkish army (Libya had for centuries been part of the Ottoman Empire). Libyans, instead of turning against the Turks, fought valiantly against the invaders, whose frustration at the drawn-out and unsuccessful campaign led them to civilian slaughter and reprisals. Italy emerged from a very bloody war with title to Libya and the Dodecanese Islands, but in return paid what amounted to an indemnity to Turkey.

13. Cesare Battisti, as a young irredentist, had been prominent in Italian aspirations to annex the southern parts of Austria. In 1916 he was captured by the Austrians in the Veneto and, since he was Austrian by birth, was executed for treason.

14. The Triple Alliance (Prussia, Austro-Hungary, Italy) was three decades old when Giolitti, past his prime, renewed it a fourth time in 1912. As war with the Triple Entente (Great Britain, France, Russia) loomed, Giolitti was a neutralist but strong nationalism on left and right favored still more national expansion. Under his successor, Antonio Salandra, Italy negotiated with Germany and Austria for more territory, and after all five of the other powers were at war concessions were promised. Salandra then approached the Entente and concluded a secret treaty promising more Austrian and Ottoman territory in return for Italy's entry on their side. The Treaty of London was signed on 26 April 1915, and Italy renounced the Alliance on 4 May.

Meanwhile, to retain Italy as an ally, Austria offered the Trentino, the Südtirol, and Trieste. Old patriot Gabriele D'Annunzio was sent round the major cities to stir up popular enthusiasm for war, because Salandra knew that national sentiment was then against entry into the conflict. Giolitti, who still controlled a majority in the Chamber of Deputies which had been told nothing of these negotiations and which was against war, came back intending to reassume the prime ministry and to undo the recent commitments. Victor Emmanuel III, however, was bent on war, and supported D'Annunzio's demagoguery. Giolitti demurred, and backed away from marshalling his parliamentary supporters. The king reappointed Salandra, and during a parliamentary recess Italy sent its army to war on 24 May, less than three weeks after it broke the Alliance.

Milani's figures on Italian dead are a reasonable estimate. Financially, the war cost more than the sum of all Italian expenditures combined since its beginning in 1861. More than 500,000 Slavs and 200,000 German-speakers found themselves enclosed within her new borders.

15. Pius X (1903–14), later canonized by Pius XII.

16. The elections of May 1921 gave the Fascists 35 seats in the Chamber of 535. Giolitti, once more premier, had helped them win even that many. Army and police troops had been told to ignore Fascist strong-arm intimidation across the land. A series of ineffectual cabinets yielded the nation to social chaos and violence. Mussolini's paramilitary black-shirts took over Ferrara, Milan,

Parma, Pisa, and a host of other cities. Then, at the end of October 1922 the Fascists embarked upon a five-day March to Rome. The armed forces in many places were already fraternizing with the black-shirts. A caretaker government was asked to call out the army; they vacillated. Then in emergency session the cabinet drew up a martial-law decree, but the King refused to sign it. Two days later Mussolini had taken over the government. The general consensus is that the Italian military forces could easily have neutralized the Fascist bands if ordered to do so.

17. This is his estimate of the death toll of World War II, and perhaps of Mussolini's other armed ventures.

18. Italy sent as many as 70,000 troops for three years in aid of General Francisco Franco's rebellion in Spain. Army regulars eventually replaced the original black-shirts. Their performance was poor, and Mussolini's hope of acquiring the Balearic Islands was given no satisfaction.

19. When General Francisco Franco led the uprising of troops against the Republic in 1936, he claimed that the Socialist government was unlawful. Although the conservative parties had received a clear majority of the popular vote at the previous election, the arrangement of electoral districts produced a parliament in the hands of their opponents.

20. Five thousand Italians, led by Liberal Socialist Carlo Rosselli, Socialist Pietro Nenni, and Communist Luigi Longo, went to fight for the Spanish Republic. Many later fought as partisans in Italy in 1944–45.

21. Milani omits to mention that Italy also declared war on and fought against Great Britain (1940) and the United States (1941).

22. Acts 5:29.

23. Concluded between Mussolini and Pius XI (1921–1939) on 11 February 1929, and commemorated on each anniversary. That holiday replaced one on 20 September, which had commemorated the seizure of Rome in 1870.

24. The letter refers to M. Clément, H. Fronsac, and P. R. Régamey, *Non-violence et objection de conscience* (Paris: Casterman, 1962). See also Régamey: *Non-Violence and the Christian Conscience* (London: Darton, Longman & Todd, 1966).

25. "Non è viltà l'obiezione di coscienza," *La Rinascita*, 6 March

1965, p. 28; see also *Politica*, 1–15 March 1965, p. 6, for a slightly different version. Borghi and his associates were also the object of much recrimination in the press, the church, and the courts.

26. The Supreme Court of Cassation is the court of highest appeal in Italy.

27. A Military Tribunal in Florence on 11 January 1963 had convicted Giuseppe Gozzini for refusing military service on grounds of conscientious objection, and a debate among Catholics ensued in the press. Don Luigi Stefani asserted (in the conservative *La Nazione*) that conscientious objection could find no justification in Catholic moral principles. The diocesan Catholic Action leadership issued a statement that they could take no position on either side of the issue, and that those who did should make clear they were expressing personal views, not church doctrine. Father Ernesto Balducci then went into print on the 13th of January with a review article in favor of conscientious objection ("The Church and the Fatherland," in *Il Giornale del Mattino*). That promptly led to his prosecution along with the editor, Leonardo Pinzauti.

The criminal complaint singled out several passages: the Church "has no rebuke for anyone whose conscience leads him to take on the burden of witness to an absolute choice for peace, by refusing, not to serve the Fatherland, but to serve it by donning its military uniform, which is always a device of war." "In the case of total war Catholics have, I would say, not the right but the duty to desert . . . The desertion of even a single citizen can be a clear enough testimony to make a decisive difference." "This gives ample grounds for us to observe a moment of silent admiration for those who give witness, at their own expense, to their absolute choice for peace."

Balducci was tried for *apologia*, or advocacy, of the crimes of desertion and military insubordination; he was acquitted on 7 March 1963 after a favorable finding of fact in the Tribunal of Florence: 6 *Rivista Italiana di Diritto e Procedura Penale* 586 (1963). The Tribunal observed, however, that the defense had argued the article was too philosophical and theoretical to have sponsored specific crimes. This very vagueness, in their opinion, made the interview's reference to total war more dangerous, for who could say precisely what a total war meant? Even if only one segment of a nation survived a nuclear attack, the judiciary would uphold the duty of its armed forces to fulfill their soldierly duties and go to war: Idem at 591.

The prosecution appealed the decision (as is possible in Italian criminal procedure) and on 15 October the Court of Appeal of Florence reversed, convicting Balducci and imposing a suspended sentence of eight months in prison: 86 *Foro Italiano* (part 2) 469 (1963). Balducci had not engaged in a simple discussion of religious ethics, the court opined; he had specifically praised a specific deserter, and had encouraged others to follow. After lengthy examination of writings by leading Vatican canonists, the Court found Balducci especially culpable for having put forward his private ideas as if they were teachings of the church, and thus misleading readers. The Court of Cassation finally affirmed on 1 June 1964: 88 Idem (part 2) 4 (1965).

28. The extracts are admittedly removed from context. Several, through omission or abbreviation, become altered in their evident meaning.

29. Dante Alighieri, *Inferno* 9:113–14. Pola (now Pula) is a Yugoslavian town at the tip of the Istrian peninsula on the Dalmatian coast, north of the Gulf of Quarnero (now Kvarner); until 1918 it had been in Austro-Hungary. Dante's allusion, because of a famous cemetery nearby, is construed here as ground for an implicit territorial claim by Italy for this presently Slavic region bordered by Trieste and Rijeka (Fiume).

30. The tomb of Count Vittorio Alfieri is in the Basilica of Santa Croce, Florence. A passionate admirer of the *literati* in eighteenth century France and England, and of popular revolution and government, he is remembered for his dramas and his autobiography.

31. *L'Unità* is the principle daily newspaper of the Italian Communist Party.

32. Each local Communist group sponsored a youth center, called a *Casa del Popolo* or People's House. Their natural competitors were the youth programs run in the local Catholic parishes, among which Don Lorenzo's stood out by its immense popularity among young workers and students.

33. The official newspaper of the Vatican. The critique appeared on 20 December 1958, very shortly after the death of Pius XII and the accession of John XXIII.

34. Quoted from Milani's *Esperienze pastorali*.

35. Many Italians had been persuaded to invest their savings in a scheme that promised extraordinarily high rates of return. The payments were made as long as increasing numbers invested, but the scheme eventually collapsed and was revealed as a swindle. The first investors came away with enormous gains, but all the rest lost their savings.

36. In 1943, when the Badoglio government which had ousted Mussolini surrendered to the Allies and instructed Italian forces to lay down their arms.

37. "La patria e don Lorenzo," *Rinascita*, 31 July 1965, p. 7.

38. Journals on either end of the ideological spectrum published fabricated interviews, which Milani did not even take the trouble to disavow: *L'Unità* on the left and *Lo Specchio* and *La Nazione* on the right.

39. "All citizens are invested with equal social status and are equal before the law, without distinction as to sex, race, language, religion, political opinions, and personal or social conditions. It is the responsibility of the Republic to remove all obstacles of an economic and social nature which, by limiting the freedom and equality of citizens, prevent the full development of the individual and the participation of all workers in the political, economic, and social organization of the country." Article 3 of the Constitution.

40. The Piave river in the Veneto was the site of a battleline held from autumn 1917 to summer 1918. A great offensive of Austrian troops failed there, with formidable losses: 35,000 dead and 100,000 wounded. Italian casualties were less than a fourth of that. The 24th of May commemorates the day of Italy's attack on Austria in 1915.

41. See note 13.

42. To justify the invasion of Poland on 1 September 1939 the Germans staged a phoney border incident with prearranged corpses, then shot their way past Polish personnel stationed there.

43. The Confederazione Italiana Sindacati Lavoratori was a federation of labor unions that combined Christian Democrats, Republicans, and Social Democrats. It played a moderate role in industrial relations, by contrast with the leftist Confederazione Generale Italiana del Lavoro (CGIL) through the 1950s, after which

the two began to make common cause. The Waldensians are a Christian church descended from the reform efforts of Pietro Valdo in the twelfth century. *La Rinascita* published a series of letters in support of Don Lorenzo; most prominent among the signers were large groups of Waldensians. For this correspondence see 10 April 1965, p. 31; 17 April, p. 31; 7 August, p. 27; 11 September, p. 26; 16 October, pp. 30–31; 6 November, pp. 34–35.

44. *Burning Conscience: The case of the Hiroshima pilot, Claude Eatherly, told in his letters to Günther Anders* (New York: Monthly Review Press, [1961]).

45. 1 Peter 2:18.

46. The final statement was as follows: "it seems just that laws should make humane provision for the use of conscientious objectors who refuse to carry arms, provided they accept some other form of community service." Vatican II, Pastoral Constitution on the Church in the Modern World (*Gaudium et Spes*) 79; *Vatican Council II: The Conciliar and Post Conciliar Documents*, ed. Austin Flannery, O.P. (New York: Pillar, 1975). This document was enacted on 7 December 1965, after Milani's "Letter to the Judges" but before his trial.

47. This is not quite accurate. Canon 141 in the *Code of Canon Law* which had gone into effect on 19 May 1918 reads:

"1. Clerics must not volunteer for service in civil armed forces, except with permission of their Ordinary [ecclesiastical superior], and even then they should resign at the earliest opportunity. Nor may they be parties to civil wars or disturbances of the public order.

"2. A minor cleric [a student in training, not yet ordained deacon or priest] who enlists contrary to the above paragraph is by that fact discharged from clerical status."

A newer *Code of Canon Law*, promulgated 25 January 1983, provides as follows: "Since military service is incongruent with the clerical state, clerics and candidates for ordination must not volunteer for armed service except with permission of their Ordinary." Canon 289:1.

48. "What Is Left to Hope For?" pp. 2–5. Born concludes his statistics: "Whoever still believes in war as a legitimate instrument of politics and clings to the traditional ideas of a hero's death for sake of wife and child and defense of the homeland should

124

now realize that these are fairy tales and not nice ones at that," p. 4.

49. (Ahmedabad: Navajivan, 1942): 1:73.

50. See *The Times* (London) 25 October 1962, 8.

51. The Tribunal is not entirely accurate. West Germany had conscription at the time, and East Germany had legalized conscientious objection in 1964.

52. The Tribunal alludes to the fact that the Fascist regime was established in Italy without any formal abrogation or radical revision in the Constitution.

53. See also the Law of 5 February 1970, no. 21.

54. Regulations in furtherance of these laws were later issued in the Decree of the Prime Minister of 26 April 1972.

55. See Gregorio, *L'obiezione di coscienza* (Turin, 1966); Coletti, *L'obiezione di coscienza* (Milan, 1973); Idem, "L'obiezione di coscienza: una legge da riformare," *Astrolabio* 31 May–30 June 1973:45ff.

56. Resolution of the General Assembly of the United Nations, 10 December 1948, ratified by Italy.

57. Signed by the Members of the Council of Europe, including Italy, 4 November 1950.

58. See a historical review of the developing jurisprudence in the Case of D. Battista, Tribunale Supremo Militare 21 February 1969: *Giustizia Penale* 1970, II, 232.

59. Defendant Amprino, T.S.M. 17 March 1972, *G.P.* 1973, II, 356; def. Trevisan, T.S.M. 30 May 1972: *G.P.* 1973, II, 363; def. Scapin, T.S.M. 30 May 1972: *G.P.* 1973, II, 364.

60. This was amended in minor ways by the Law of 21 May 1974, no. 249, and by the Law of 24 December 1974, no. 695. Regulations in furtherance of the law were issued in the Circular no. 500081/30, of 5 November 1974 by the Minister of Defense, and in the Decree of the President of the Republic of 28 November 1977, no. 1139.

61. Defendant Bellassai, Tribunale Supremo Militare 13 April 1973: *G.P.* 1973, II, 354.